Meet Tony

a memoir by

Don Conover

To our great good
friends Don & Alice
Best Wishes
Don & Bobbie

ISBN 1552123596

9 781552 123591

Don Conover

130 Marjory Lane

Sequim, Washington 98382

(360) 683-6985

Cover by Marie Conover

conoverm@hotmail.com

Canadian Cataloguing in Publication Data

Conover, Don
  Meet Tony

  ISBN 1-55212-359-6

  1. Conover, Don, 1916- 2. Alaska--Biography. 3. World War,
1939-1945--Personal narratives, American. I. Title.
F910.7.C66A3 2000   979.8'05'092   C00-910327-9

TRAFFORD

This book was published on-demand in cooperation with Trafford Publishing.
On-demand publishing is a unique process and service of making a book available for
retail sale to the public taking advantage of on-demand manufacturing and Internet mar-
keting.
On-demand publishing includes promotions, retail sales, manufacturing, order fulfil-
ment, accounting and collecting royalties on behalf of the author.

Suite 6E, 2333 Government St., Victoria, B.C. V8T 4Z1, CANADA
Phone   250-383-6864   Toll-free 1-888-232-4444 (Canada & US)
Fax   250-383-6804   E-mail   sales@trafford.com
Web site www.trafford.com trafford publishing is a division of trafford holdings ltd.
Trafford Catalogue #00-0001   www.trafford.com/robots/00-0001.html

10   9   8   7   6   5   4   3   2

A guy once told me "You should write a book!" I did.

I want to thank my wife, Bobbie, for riding out my wild ideas with me, my daughter Pattie for her help in taming the computer, the moral support of my sons Dale, Robert, and Russell. Daughter Linda for formatting and Marie for the great cover and book design. She took a simple photo furnished by Clare and Phil Ballard and worked her magic on it.

1. Bobbie, Don and Kenai—Resupply Mission

2. Our home on the Homestead

3. Don, Russ, Bob, Pattie, and Dale taking

   a Swimming Break

4. Eight Three Mike—our airliner

5. Water Brigade

6. Ted and Don before Rhine Mission

7. "Any landing you can walk away from..."

The horselaugh is from Tony's spirit, coming back from horse heaven or wherever he is, for all the things he put me through. His freedom as a wild mustang was interrupted for three years by me, dogs, kids, cars, a barn, ropes, saddle, bridle, firecrackers and a Fourth of July parade. It's okay. After seventy years, I still miss him.

Part One

Utah 1926–1935
Before Tony

Liberty Bell Bank

I was only 6 years old, and afraid this giant was going to pull me apart just like I had done to that butterfly. It was 1922 and I was being introduced to terror. I couldn't sleep, couldn't think of anything—except that great big jolly man. But he wouldn't be jolly when he found out what I had done. He would kill me. Wish I hadn't done it. It was just an accident that I heard him. The other guy said, "How much do you weigh then?"

"I'm six feet seven and weigh 322."

"Glad I'm not feedin' ya!"

Snick and I had gone to the Star Theater Vaudeville and Matinee to see Tom Mix and Tony ridin' and shootin' up the bad guys. 'Fore, that though, was the vaudeville act of "Man Mountain Kersey." Mr. Kersey sang, told stories and danced around. Really good for a "Man Mountain." (He sings! He dances! He entertains! For one week only. Don't Miss It!)

We were just fooling around after the matinee. The big guy and his partner were on the stage re-arranging stuff. Snick and I were the last ones out of the theater. I heard talking. Don't think Snick did. He wasn't payin' 'tenshun I guess.

So what was the problem? Well, there was a contest put on by the Bank of Tintic. The kid who guessed closest to Mr. Kersey's weight would win a Chrome Plated Liberty Bell savings bank. The guesses were to be turned into the box office by Thursday noon. The award would be at the Saturday matinee. The Mayor would be there; the bank President would present the award.

"Should I, or shouldn't I" I asked myself. Yes or No. It was cheatin'. I wanted to win. "What would Mom and Dad think?" Worst part, what would Mr. Kersey do? Did he know I heard him? Snick hadn't heard. Hadn't said a word about it. Now I knew about agony.

Wednesday I turned in my guess. I didn't want to be too high or too low. Couldn't let some guy sneak in. I wrote 323 on the card, signed it and turned it in.

Now I was really worried. Couldn't sleep. Had nightmares about Mr. Kersey holdin' me up to his face and growlin' "Smart kid, eh! I'll fix your wagon!"

Just about decided not to go to the awards, when the Eureka Reporter came out with the story. "Amazing guess by young Don Conover. Only one pound away from the true weight of Man Mountain Kersey."

Now I had to go get that lousy bank. "GEE!"

"You're not eating your supper. Don't you feel well?" That was Mom.

"I'm just fine." I wasn't.

Award night and mom had me shined up. Hair combed, pants and coat pressed. Even a damned necktie! She took me down to the theater and we sat through the singin', dancin' and then the cowboy part. I wriggled and squirmed. Hated every second of it. The lights came on, the drummer and the piano woke everybody up, then came the ceremony. The bank guy made a speech about saving pennies when you're a kid and you'll wind up with dollars when you've growed up.

I stood there between him and the monster. Couldn't look at him. Just stood there and shook.

"And the amazing guess by young Mr. Conover is only one pound over the weight of Man Mountain Kersey, so we are delighted to award to him this beautiful replica of our nation's Liberty Bell. Remember, saving will bring you liberty!"

As I took the bell from him, Kersey reached over, grabbed me by both arms and sat me on his shoulder. It was all I could do to keep from peein'. He danced around the stage with me just sittin' there. Finally he set me back down on the stage. I took off, ran down the steps, up the aisle, out the door and all the way home.

Mom asked me, several times later, "Whatever possessed you to act that way, son?"

I just shrugged.

Meet Tony

Tony and I had a three-year contest. I owned Tony, but he didn't know that. I was ten years old; Tony was just over two. I weighed sixty pounds; Tony weighed six hundred. At first, he was scared; I was petrified. We shared fear.

I had wanted a horse for a year or two. Dad said no, for a number of reasons. There was no place to pasture, hay was expensive, we had no barn, we lived in a high mountain pass in Utah, no place for a horse. I kept pestering and finally my brother, Dean said, "If you can trade my Indian motorcycle for a horse, you can have it. The motorcycle was a one-speed, one-cylinder rig you had to push to start. Dean had got it from the dump and worked on it 'til he got it running.

The Planter brothers brought mustangs in from the desert, trained them, then sold them to the University of Utah for use as polo ponies. Jack agreed to swap a horse for the bike. Dad, now, entered the discussions. He picked out a gentle, four-year-old mare. Before we made the swap, I was hanging around their corral one day. They were just bringing in a batch of mustangs. I spotted Tony. I was entranced. He was Tony, because he was black, had a blaze face and three white stockings, just like my hero, Tom Mix's "Tony." I told the cowboys. "That's the horse I want!" That was okay with them.

Bringing Tony to the barn next door was a wild, exciting experience. I found out later that the only time Tony had felt a rope, 'til then, was when they snipped his jewels. Now he was one violent, unforgiving Gelding. My brother, Clyde, one hundred and eighty pounds, and his buddy Burt each had a rope on

Tony. He fought being led and when we got far enough into town to where there were houses, kids, cars, dogs, and people, he pulled the handlers all over the street. Frantic, snorting, wild-eyed, rearing, he was almost too much for the two of them. Finally, after an exhausting hour or more, they were able to get him into the barn and slam the door.

Dad was furious because we had brought Tony instead of the mare. "Damn it, don't you ever mind?" Mom helped to smooth it over and I kept Tony.

Clyde decided to teach Tony to lead. So he tied the halter rope to the car bumper and led him around for a while. When they untied him he reared up and struck Burt on the forearm with his hoof, peeling most of the hide off. Could have killed old Burt.

Dad decided to hire a cowboy to rough break Tony, which he did. Right after the cowboy worked with Tony, and before I had even ridden him, I decided that carrying water for his drinking tub was too much work. I would lead him the block and a half, to "Horseturd" Morgan's Livery Stable, where there was a watering trough for his horses. Tony was skittish, but I managed to pull and lead him there.

I certainly hadn't expected an audience would greet me, but as we pulled up to the water, several of my school chums gathered round to watch and needle me.

"Why don'tcha ride him?" "Are you chicken?" "Some cowboy!" "Let's see you get on him!" Tony had pulled back from the trough and was getting jumpy from all the noise. I looked at my hecklers with supreme contempt and went over to shinny up Tony's front leg. As I put my hand on his withers, he whirled, knocked me down, stepped on the back of my neck and took off for the hills.

Dad would have let him go, but Tony had the halter and the rope on. Dad was afraid he would get the rope caught and starve to death, so he hired a cowboy, for ten bucks, to go bring him in.

After my neck healed and Tony was back in the barn, my sometimes-bruising education continued. The top priority now was to get a saddle and bridle. Luckily we found a neat, kid's saddle with shiny brass spots on the skirt, and matching bridle, of course. Next came the cowboy boots. Dad would not spring for new ones. I finally found a pair of badly used ones. The toes were worn through from dragging through the gravel playing. Playing marbles, I guess. The shoemaker capped them over the toes. Now I was all set.

Clyde had an old crowbait mare. She was a lot more gentle than Tony, so Dad persuaded Clyde to swap horses with me 'til Tony got a little less rambunctious. It worked out that I got Tony back after a few weeks.

Step by step, I worked with Tony, until he would do pretty much what I wanted. After a while I could saddle, bridle, and curry him, all that cowboy stuff. Tony was never a pet. He was a challenge. If you shinnied up his leg he would reach around and bite your butt. He'd back away when you tried to get your foot in the stirrup. If you got on him close to the barn, he would de-skin your leg on the rough barn siding before you could get control. He would try to rub you off by ducking under tree limbs. He would dart into side alleys, either leaving you flying in the original direction, or hanging onto his mane and the saddle horn. He could put you sitting in the air, alongside the saddle, if he saw a snake. You had to belt him in the belly or he'd bloat and leave you with a slack cinch and a slippery saddle. He would kick, but seldom buck. Right from the first though, Mom could walk right up to Tony, give him a carrot or a sugar lump with no problem. No one ever really owned Tony.

After a few months it got so that I would take a lunch, Tony, and our dog Teddy, and we would be gone all day, roaming the hills. There was a grove of Aspen down toward the valley, up and over the hill from the limestone quarry. I guess that was my favorite place. We would get there about noon. I would put a rope on Tony, loosen the cinch, and take off the bridle so he could graze. We would all drink from a nice spring. I would eat my lunch. We would all take it easy. I would lay on the grass, look up through the quaking leaves and dream of all kinds of neat things. On a nice day that was the best place in the world.

My first bareback ride was on a day that vanished from my memory. Tony and I had been up to Knightsville, maybe showing off a little, yah know, bareback. We were a couple of blocks from home on the return trip, when (I was told later) a page of newspaper, carried by the forever wind of that valley, blew up and was held against Tony's forelegs. They tell me he really went wild, threw me to the gravel road and took off. One of the witnesses grabbed the reins, others helped me up and they all escorted Tony and me to my house. Mother dressed the gravel scrapes, then put me to bed. I was conscious, but out of my head. They said I would repeat myself when I talked. "Hello Burt, howya doin'?" A couple of minutes later, "Hello Burt. Howya doin'?" Next day I could not remember anything that happened the previous day. Still cannot.

One of my favorite spots in the hills, was Cole Canyon cliffs, right at the valley's edge. There was enough water so some grass was mixed in with the juniper and pine trees. Wild horses would come in from the desert. Someone, probably the Planter brothers, had built an elaborate corral. The long wing fences of wire, packed with tumbleweeds to make a solid wall, were used to guide the wild mustangs into the regular pole corral.

My buddy, Bill, and I used that corral one time to catch a little crippled mare. She was with a herd of mustangs but couldn't keep up with them if they were spooked. We ran her into the corral and put a rope on her. She was not wild so we could look at her leg without getting our heads kicked off. The ankle was swollen, big as a cantaloupe, with an inch wide ring of blood and pus going clear around her leg. Bill got down for a better look.

"Geez! It looks like there is a horseshoe in there. I can see the ends."

Stray Pound

I can just hear my Dad saying, "Hell, my kid can do that." He must have been talking to some of the city fathers and the subject of stray animals came up. Seems the city needed someone to gather up the stray horses and cattle that were a nuisance around town. Dad suggested me, I guess, cause I got the job. Dad had insisted that I do something to help pay for the hay, barn and other costs of keeping Tony. I was eleven years old and on call twenty-four hours a day. I was paid fifty cents a head for every animal I brought in.

One day I got a call about some cattle that were causing trouble up on Church Street, so I got on Tony and went after them. There were seven in the bunch, once I got them all rounded up and headed down the road. We didn't have any trouble until we got to Main Street.

We came down the hill by Morgan's Livery Stable on the corner. The Stray Pound was one-half block down Main Street and behind the City Hall building on the other side of the street. I rode ahead to see if I could drive them down Main, otherwise, I would have to cross the street, drive them an extra three blocks and come into the Pound from the back.

Main was clear so I turned them down it. I was thinking about my three dollars and fifty cents, when a car came up the street and worked its way through the cattle. At the same time a group of, well dressed, ladies were forced to mingle with the four cattle that the car had driven onto the sidewalk.

Tony and I were on the other side of the street, in front of a furniture store with great big plate glass windows. Three of the cattle were crowded into the recessed, glass entryway. It all got pretty noisy with the women shrieking and hollering cause they couldn't get back in the Elks Club building. More women were coming out.

It got worse—a guy in a bright red roadster, with a cutout on his exhaust, came roaring up the street and stopped just at the entrance to the City Hall. He was impatient, so kept revving the engine. About then it was noisier than hell and Tony was getting frantic.

I'm trying to get this all straightened out when a heifer bolted back up the street. I chased her down and brought her back. She was worth four bits to me. When I got back the manager of the store was at the door yelling at me.

"See all this glass kid. Get these damned animals away before they go through a window!" Mrs. Ostrander (head of the Lady Elks) was screaming at me from the other side of the street.

I couldn't get the cattle to move because of the red roadster. I yelled, "Hey you, back up!" He didn't pay any attention.

"Son, what are you trying to do?" Out of the bedlam, a friendly voice.

"Mister, I'm the City Stray Pound manager. The Pound is back of the City Hall and the cattle are afraid of that roadster."

"Jack," my friend called to his buddy. "Get that guy to back up. These cattle have to go into the city yard.

" They got the roadster backed up and the guy even shut down the engine. The only sound then, was the chattering of the women, as my friend and Jack helped Tony and me separate the cattle from the Elk.

Once I got the strays in the city driveway I was all set. I put them in the pen, checked in with the city clerk and left by the back way. Later I got a check for three-fifty, and copies of letters to the Mayor from Mrs. Ostrander and Taylor Brothers Furniture Store.

Parade

Tony and I were going to be in a parade. Tony didn't know this. Nobody knew this but me, and I could keep a secret. The circus was coming to town. It had a big Wild West Show with cowboys, Indians, and stagecoaches. Neat, neat stuff. Of course, they advertised that the big parade would start July 4th at 10 AM.

Wearing a clean yellow shirt, clean Levis, polished boots, new bandana, and a shined leather band on my hat, I was ready. Early on the morning of the fourth, I had polished the brass on the saddle and bridle; saddle soaped the leather, and then took Tony down to Morgan's Watering Trough where I gave him a complete bath. I then rubbed him down with a towel, curried him and combed his mane and tail. Tony glistened and glowed— Beautiful. At ten o'clock Tony and I were at Henroid's Grocery, back from Main Street, waiting.

First came the elephant with the pretty lady sitting on its head. Then came wagons with lions and tigers. Next a big Calliope with its jazzy music and behind it, more performers. Finally came a stagecoach with Indians on horses behind it. Now I could see the cowboys. There were five of them. What a sight they made with their beautiful, tooled cowboy boots, tight pant legs tucked into the tops. All wore colorful shirts, leather-jeweled vests, neckerchiefs and big ten-gallon Stetson hats, some black, some white.

You could tell that the horses had practiced prancing. Their necks were arched, head back, tail raised, lifting their fore legs. They seemed to be in tune with the music. With silver on their saddles, bridles and martingales flashing, they just looked grand.

"Excuse me please, I have to get through," I said, as I worked Tony through the crowd to the street.

The cowboys were two, two, and one, with the one on the left so I just eased Tony in alongside him. He was surprised to see me and said, "Get outta here kid! Beat it! Scram! "

I acted like I didn't hear him.

We continued on down the street with him yelling at me, but I was too busy trying to control Tony to pay much attention. Tony was really getting to be a handful. The noise of the calliope, the crowd shouting, was making ol' Tony mighty frisky. He was taking short jumpy steps, throwing his head around. His eyes were big and his nostrils wide. It wasn't at all like I thought it would be.

The worst part was that it was too late to get out of it. The crowd was right up to the edge of the parade. Now the street narrowed, the crowd was thicker, the sound intense. I could feel Tony trembling. I wasn't steady, myself. I didn't know what to expect. I just had to be ready.

We passed Dad's garage. He was the Ford Dealer. I could tell, by the look he threw me, that I would have some listening to do later.

When we passed Morgan's Livery Stable, I was stuck cause that was the last road on my side and it was jammed with people. I couldn't take Tony through all those people. I couldn't take him into a crowd.

Someone threw a firecracker. Tony reared, almost going over backward. He came down, squatting his rump, skittered back, and slammed into the shoulder of the cowboy's horse. I heard some profanity, so I kicked Tony in the ribs. We moved away. I was standing in the stirrups, leaning forward, with both arms straight, my fists in Tony's mane. Good thing I was, because when he threw his head back, he just brushed my face with his mane. We were all over our small area. Tony was getting wilder by the minute. More firecrackers, waving flags, brilliant parasols bobbing and people shouting: "Look at the kid!"

"Atta boy Don. You're doing great!" We were the star attraction, I guess.

The cowboys were still cussing me to get the hell out of there, but I had no place to go. I was ready, that's for sure, but it was all I could do to stay in the saddle. The whole parade, for me, was what's next? Be ready!

The crowd finally thinned out some. There was Church Street. I saw an opening in the crowd and worked Tony through it. As soon as we were in the open road, Tony took out like his tail was on fire. We were running up hill but going so fast that I didn't dare try to turn him onto Leadville Street. I just enjoyed the wild free ride ol' Tony was giving me.

He finally wound down. We ambled around through the sagebrush and gullies, then back to the barn. "Damn. That was a fine day!"

Midnight

We were on our way to Dry Valley, where the wild horse corral was. I was trying to describe, to Bill, the fight between the stallions that Tony, Teddy and I had seen there. We had been ringside of the thrilling, brutal contest. The dozen, or so, mares had been grazing, peacefully, with the black stallion off to one side. We saw a big, bay horse working its way, through the brush toward them.

The black stallion snorted and we all came to attention.

The two horses came together. As soon as they were close enough, they reared, striking at each other with their front legs, manes and tails flying, teeth bared, the huge muscles in their shoulders and thighs, rippling and flexing with effort. They put on a terrifying spectacle. They would come down, whirl, kick two or three times, then back up, rearing and sparring. All this was punctuated by the shrieking, grunting, thudding noise of their combat. Their hoofs, like edged clubs, brought blood from rips and tears in their hides. A short breather and they lunged at each other again. The bay, finally faltered, so the stallion whirled and planted two rib-cracking kicks to his chest. The bay turned tail and ran away. The stallion chased him only a short distance then rushed back to the mares, prancing in triumph.

"I sure wish you could have seen it. They were going at it like crazy. The stallion finally beat the bay up pretty bad."

We hung around the spring for a while, had our sandwiches and pop, and then headed back for town. We hadn't seen any horses, deer or anything, just jackrabbits and sagehens. As we came over the ridge by Cole Canyon cliffs, we saw the big, black stallion.

"Bill," I said, "that might be him, you know, the one I was telling you about. Where's the mares?" We stopped and looked around. He was alone, just grazing. We eased forward and when closer, I said. "That's not him. That stallion was all cut up. This one has no scars. Ain't it a beaut!"

"Maybe we could run him back to the corral, and catch him. He ain't branded."

"We could, but even if we got him in there, we have only one lariat. We couldn't hold him. Isn't he something?"

The stallion was not paying much attention to us. He just kept his distance as we walked along. We weren't herding—just hazing him along at a walk.

First thing you know we could see Knightsville, then the ball field. Just to the left of that, a quarter mile or so, was Fennel's slaughterhouse.

"Bill, I said, We might be able to get him into Fennel's corral."

"Yeah, let's try it!"

"I'll go off to the right, try to get ahead of him. (Tony was faster than Bill's big, old King was.) If the gate is open we will try to turn him in!"

Tony and I dropped into a gully, then trotted and galloped toward town. When I was a ways ahead of the stallion, I cut back towards him, circling in front of him. Bill kept coming and was able to bring him right in front of the corral.

The gate was open.

We had never done anything to make him skittish so our unexpected closing in on him worked exactly as we had hoped. He darted through the gate and was in the corral. I followed him in and Bill blocked the gate, then closed it.

"Damn, we got him! Now what?"

"We've got ourselves one big, black stallion!"

We watched as he trotted around checking things out. We could see that he didn't like this new place at all.

"I think he could jump out of here," Bill said. The fence was about five feet high, with three strands of barbed wire.

"Yeah, or he might run into the bobwire and cut himself up."

There was a pen, about twenty feet square, where the Fennels bunched the cattle before prodding them through a chute to be slaughtered. It was strongly built of two by twelve lumber and was over six feet high. The gate was open.

"Let's get him in there," I said.

"Okay."

We closed in on him again, got him in, and slammed the gate. He was really frantic now, running around and around, rearing and snorting and shrieking. He tried to jump the fence, but fell back in.

"Let's get back away before he hurts himself."

We were thrilled, but scared, by what we had done.

"Let's pull some grass and put it in there. We can come back in the morning with some help."

We pulled some grass, then went home for supper.

I took care of Tony, then burst through our kitchen door.

"Mom! Bill and I caught a big, black stallion. He's out at Fennel's slaughterhouse corral. We've got to find out about getting a brand for Bill and me, so he'll be ours."

"You better talk to your Dad about this, I don't know—"

At supper I tried to get my brothers to promise to help me with the stallion, but they all had things to do. Dad didn't come home 'til late so I couldn't talk to him.

That night I was too excited to sleep. I tried to figure out a brand, then there was the big job of choosing a name. Midnight? I had heard that ebony meant black. How about Ebony? Bill would have to agree. How would we break him and tame him down. After a while I went to sleep and dreamt of winning the big race at the county fair on Midnight.

At Breakfast—

"We sure as hell don't need another horse!" Dad speaking.

"By the time I get someone to break him, get another saddle and bridle, have him shod, I'd have put out a lot of money. You've got Tony, that's enough!"

"But Dad, he's a beautiful horse. Bill and I worked hard to catch him. He's ours. After a while, maybe, we could sell him for a lot of money."

"I know you are excited. I can't imagine how you caught him. Hard to believe two kids could do that!"

"You come out to Fennel's and you'll see. You can't help but like him!"

"I have to meet some people, but I'll drive out about ten."

"Thanks Dad, we'll be out there."

I called Bill and told him I couldn't get any help, but that my Dad was going out later.

We were excited and had picked up a few friends on our way through town. We were bragging about our big, old stallion. These guys wanted to see him.

As we neared the corral we couldn't see the stallion. Soon we were close enough to see that the gate was open. We galloped in and saw that the pen gate was also open and that Midnight was gone.

We were stunned and heart broken. How could this happen?

"I think you guys are full of baloney. You never caught no stallion!"

We couldn't even answer. We went into the pen.

"See those horse tracks," Bill shouted. "What do you think made them? Do they look like deer tracks? Somebody let him out!"

"After all our work. Damn them, whoever they are."

Bill and I took off on our horses and left our "friends" to walk back. We were crushed and had a hard time to keep from crying. We could not believe Midnight was gone.

I caught Dad and told him he didn't have to go out.

"Some bastard turned him loose!"

Dad raised his hand, I started to duck, but he stopped it and let it drop on my shoulder.

"I'm sorry Don. I know you're disappointed. Probably some kids did it."

We Get Fired

Dad said that some kids probably turned Midnight loose. Maybe he was back in the hills.

The next day I rode clear back out to have one more look. I went to Dry Valley. I didn't see Midnight or any other horses.

A couple of days later I decided to have one more look. I went to Dry Valley, then came back a different way. This time I passed right by the Planters corral, where I had gotten Tony. They had a big black horse in there, so I rode closer. It was Midnight! He had a fresh brand on his rump. It was he, all right! I just went numb. That was why I couldn't find him in the hills. That's where he had gone. He was stolen and branded!

"I gotta tell Dad!"

Racing home I thought about it. My brother, Dean, had gotten the one-lunger bike back. Jack had crashed into the brush with it. He told Dean where the bike was, and that Dean could have it back for ten dollars.

Jack had been bitten by the motorcycle bug and had gone to Salt Lake and bought a new Harley. A couple of weeks ago Jack had tried to ride the Harley after a few drinks, had piled it up and broken his hip. Jack was still in the hospital, so the thief had to be his brother, Tom. Tom must have seen us bring Midnight in to the Fennels.

I jumped off Tony, tied him, and then rushed into Dad's office.

"Dad! Dad! I've found Midnight! He's in Planters corral. Tom stole him from us and he's branded him. Branded Midnight! Let's get him arrested. He stole our horse!"

"Calm down now, calm down. Give me this again—slower!"

"Dad, I've been lookin' for Midnight, yah know, in the hills. Couldn't find him 'til today. I came by Planters corral. I saw this big, black horse so I went closer. It was Midnight. He has a new brand on his rump. Planters brand!"

"I'll be damned. You're sure?"

"Of course I'm sure. I can get Bill and we can prove it. Let's get him arrested!"

"Hold on. Let's think about this." Dad turned away, put his hand to his chin, scratched his whiskers then said, "Did anyone see you bring that horse in from the hills?"

"N--- No, just Bill and I. We didn't see anyone else."

"In all that time, driving it in, you saw no one?"

"Yup, never saw anyone. Come on; let's go tell the sheriff. He's got the horse!"

"Don, we have to be able to prove it's your horse. How are we going to do that?"

"Why should we have to prove it. Midnight belongs to us. Bill and me! He stole it from us, has him in his corral. Let's go get him!"

"Well, young man. It's not that simple. They're going to deny it."

"It's Tom, Dad. Jack's in the hospital."

"Oh! That's right, I heard about that. You go out and play and I'll think about it."

"We want him back, Dad. He's ours."

"I know, we'll see."

At supper, "DAD, what are we going to do about Midnight?"

"I don't think we can do anything. Tom has the horse. It has his brand. We have no way of proving that you boys caught him."

"Bill and I can tell him how we caught Midnight."

"The sheriff will not take the word of two kids against a tax-paying adult. Even if he did, it would have to go to court. The Judge would want credible witnesses—adults."

"It's not fair. Midnight belongs to us. Not him!"

"No, it's not fair, Don, but you still have Tony. Tom could say that catching wild horses is his business, that no kids could bring in a big horse like that."

"Well we did! I'm going up there and turn him loose!"

"No you are not. Don't go off half cocked. They wouldn't hesitate to arrest you. You just have to face facts. He has your horse and is going to keep him. Now that's the end of it."

Eventually I got over the loss of Midnight. I still hated Tom and took great satisfaction in running his stray animals into the pound. I don't know why he let so many of his horses wander around town, but I was costing him up to three dollars a week in pound bills. Tom had one little black and white pinto, hobbled on the front legs, which I put in the pound, several times. That horse could jump fences and run like a deer even with those hobbles.

One day Dad said, "Don, you've been fired from the pound job."

"I have? Why did they do that?"

"Tom Planter told them you were going out into the foothills and bringing his horses into the pound."

"That's a lie!"

"Well, that's what he told them. They believed him."

"Well, anyway, you don't have to round up the strays anymore. They gave the job to Tom."

"I can't understand why I can't just go and tell them the truth."

"Oh yes! They said something about a couple of letters, one from Mrs. Ostrander and another from Taylor Brothers Furniture Store...something about cattle on Main Street."

"Oh that!"

"Don, you just have to forget and accept what has happened. Welcome to the real world!"

Tony and the Famous Lady

Folks around town were talking about this famous aviatrix. I had read in the Eureka Reporter that her airplane had cracked up on landing at the McEntire's Ranch. The paper said that she was trying to fly clear across the United States, from New York to California. She was staying with the rich owners of the Chief Consolidated Mine. Had been there for a month or more, waiting for parts for her airplane.

Every time I saw her she was wearing light colored men's type pants, a leather jacket and, sometimes, a white scarf. She had short, kinda reddish hair, a big smile and freckles. She walked around town a lot, getting her exercise, I guess.

Tony and I were coming down Leadville Street and met her coming the other way.

"Hi!" she said, "That's a nice pony."

"He's a mustang," I said, "name's Tony. Was wild when I got him."

"What's your name?"

"Don."

"Well Don, I'm Amelia and I think Tony has a problem. What's wrong with his nose?"

"I don't know. Mom gave me some Mentholatum to put on it, but it isn't getting any better."

"Well, I know something about horses. Jump down."

I slid off the horse and she picked up Tony's foreleg. Then worked his hoof back and forth.

"Don, look down in his fetlock. See the festering sores down in there?"

I looked and sure enough it was bloody, pussey and dirty.

"What's happening here, is that you are not keeping the floor of the barn clean. When you have an animal you have to take good care of it. You are not and it's a shame. Tony has been standing around in that wet manure. It has caused an infection in his fetlocks. He tries to scratch it with his nose, so that gets infected too. Either take care of him or give him to someone who will!"

"Yes Ma'am, I will."

"Ask your mother to get some salt pork, then you melt it down in a pan. After it cools, it will be thick grease. You take that grease and rub it on Tony's nose and in his fetlocks, but first, CLEAN THE BARN!"

"Yes ma'am, I will."

"I'm not trying to be mean. I just can't stand to see animals abused."

"I'll do what you say, right away."

"This is a great place to have a horse. I know you must have a lot of fun with Tony."

"I do. Ma'am, the paper says you are flying across the country."

"That's what I'm doing, but right now I'm waiting for a propeller. It has to come from England and must be carved and tested before they can ship it. It takes a long time."

"Isn't it scary to fly like that. Tony and I saw a plane take the steeple off the town hall and then crash into a brick wall of Taylor Brothers Furniture Store. It hit up high, then fell to the ground. Casey Jones was killed, and his girlfriend was hurt bad. The pilot, in the back seat, jumped out and was OK."

"I heard about that. This is high country, 6500 feet. Airplanes don't climb too well at this altitude. He should have circled and climbed higher before coming up the valley. He was trying to get too many rides in. It happens."

"The plane was an Alexander Eaglerock. I saw it on the tail."

"My airplane is a Parasol, made in England."

"Why is it called a Parasol? That's a funny name."

"The top wing is extra high above the fuselage, so I guess somebody thought it looked like a Parasol."

"Aren't you afraid of getting lost?"

"If the weather is bad, I don't fly, and, of course, I have a compass. Do you understand a compass?"

"Yeah, it points north, I know that."

"It points to magnetic north, so at night it wouldn't point to the North Star."

"Why not?"

"Because the magnetic pole is east of the North Pole. The difference is called variation. You have to take that into consideration, when navigating. There is also deviation, which is caused by the iron in the engine pulling on the needle."

"Wow! You sure have to be smart to fly across the country. I could never do that."

"Yes you could, when you get a little older."

"Don, have you ever been to McEntire's ranch, where I landed?"

"Oh sure, we know those folks."

"What did you see when you were there?"

"Well they got those great big silos, a nice big house, windmills, cattle, everything."

"What else is near there?"

"There's a depot and a railroad."

"Can you see the railroad from up on the mountain?"

"Oh yes, I can see it easy."

"Okay, now, this is our secret—I can see it from the air, too. It goes all the way across the United States! Works a lot better than a compass."

"Good bye Don, you take good care of Tony."

"I sure will. Thanks. G'bye."

Moonshiners

Bill and I were rabbit hunting. So far we had a big Jack and two Cottontails. We were sittin' under a pine tree, having a smoke. I had brought a piece of the Reporter paper, so we rolled some cedar bark between our hands. When it was fluffed up, we rolled it in the newspaper, licked it shut, then twisted one end, put the other end in our mouths and lit them. It didn't taste too good, but it was a smoke. The horses were grazing, What a spot! Beautiful!

"This would be a good place to come for pine nuts."

"Yeah, we could get a whole gunny sack right here."

"We'll come back next month. I can't wait to have some. When we put them in the oven you can smell them all over the house."

"I know, dig em out when the cone pops open, that's when they're good, still hot and juicy."

"Hey you guys!" It was Snick and Toby from Dutchtown. They were hustling up to where we were. They had a twenty-two, but no rabbits.

"You better stay away from there!" Toby pointed toward a hill. "We just got shot at!"

"Why?"

"I dunno, we were just hunting and this guy yelled at us to stay away, then took a shot!"

"Must be crazy!"

"Were gettin' outta here!" They left.

Bill and I got on our horses, then sort of headed toward town, but away from where they had pointed. That's for sure!

The big news, next day, was about how the cops had arrested this foreigner guy. He had a still out there. Made moonshine, so had scared Toby and Slick away.

My older brother, Dean, had told me all about bootlegging. In fact, sometimes, their bunch would go out and raid a still and then they would all get drunk. I remember when I was six, or so, taking a jug over my elbow and having a snort with them. They all got a big kick out of that.

The foreigner guy was a friend of a German family, who owned a bakery, so they were able to get him out on bail.

About a week later we heard that the guy had committed suicide. Put a pistol in his mouth and pulled the trigger. What had happened was that his fingerprints matched those of an escaped prisoner who had run away from California twenty years ago.

Paul and I sneaked into the Undertakers, just two houses up from my Dad's garage. We saw the body. The lid was up on the coffin. He looked real nice. Up close, you could see that the back of his head was gone.

There sure was a lot of talk about moonshiners for a while. They told about a practically brand new still that was stolen from the Sheriff's office. The window wasn't even broken. Must have had a key.

Our favorite bootlegger was a guy named Pete. He had this big fancy, touring car. The body was shaped like a boat, sorta. It was a beautiful, shiny tan and had a lot of chrome on the running boards, headlights, radiator and bumpers. There was a white canvas top. Pete would take us kids down to Warm Creek to swim. The word would get around, "Be on Main Street at ten-o'clock."

We would be standing there and Pete would come in his great big car, picking kids up all the way to the Summit. I was lucky one time. I got to ride the fender. You would sit behind the big, chrome headlight, wrap your legs around it, and hang on.

Pete would take us down The Slant at about seventy. The wind would have blown me off without my legs around the headlight. The fifteen miles to Warm Creek was a windy, heart thumping ride. Pete would leave us off at the millpond, warning us that he would be back in a couple of hours.

The folks said that Pete had the fastest car and the biggest gas tank in the country so, when he was carrying booze, he would just outrun the cops. My Dad thought that Pete was making a booze run when he carried us kids.

We would have a keen time, skinny dipping, then be ready when Pete came back to take us home.

The Mayor, of our town, was picked up in Lyndal, about forty miles away. He was driving our city garbage truck, with a whole bunch of booze in the back. I just hoped they kept him locked up for a long time. He was the chief guy that believed Sam Planter, about me bringing in Sam's horses from the foothills and putting them in the Stray Pound. He believed that liar and now he was paying for his sins.

Picnic

"A whole bunch of girls are going on a picnic, out by Cole Canyon Cliffs." Bill said.

" Who are they?"

"Taffy, Bernice, Ruth, all them gals."

"Let's go out and sneak up on them and eat their lunch..."

"Yeah! Let's."

We found out where they were going to be, rode to the hill behind their camp, tied up our horses. We were going to crawl up and snatch their lunch. We didn't have to do that. When we peeked over the hill, they were out picking up rocks and shells, shattering like a bunch of magpies.

It was real easy to sneak into their camp, pick out a couple sandwiches, two bottles of pop and get back to the horses.

We ate the lunch, then rode a big circle and came in over the flats, back to their camp.

Real smooth, Bill said, "Hi there, having a picnic?"

They did some giggling then asked, "Where have you guys been?"

Taking my time, throwing a leg over the saddle horn, I said, "We been out to Dry Valley, looking for some mustangs to run in."

"There were none around," Bill said. "We saw you gals at the spring, so came over."

I saw Bernice and Ruth talking and giggling. Pretty soon, Bernice came over.

"Don, Ruth wants me to ask a favor."

"Yeah, what?"

"She wants to ride back to town with you."

"Geez! She does?" I'd had a crush on Ruth for a long time.

"Yes, she tore the seat out of her gym bloomers and doesn't want to walk through town that way."

"Oh!"

"Could she do that?"

I looked over at Ruth, but she had her head down.

"Yeah, I guess so."

Bill was over talking to Taffy. Bernice went back to Ruth and they came walking over, coming up behind Tony.

I took my foot out of the stirrup. Ruth stepped in and swung up behind me. She grabbed me around the chest. I liked that a lot.

Taffy had told Bill, I guess, cause he said, "I'll see you later."

I headed Tony toward town, but I wasn't about to gallop in and get this over with.

Her arms kinda choked up my throat, so she did most of the talking. She went on about her dancing, music. She was taking private lessons. The trip to Yellowstone they were going on, all that stuff.

We were, suddenly in town and were getting near her house.

"Would you go to the matinee at the Star Theater, on Saturday, with me?" I finally got it out.

"Oh! I'll have to ask my parents."

"Okay."

I stopped at her gate and she slid off.

"Thanks a lot. I'll call you."

I never looked back, just ran old Tony back to the barn. She called later, said it was all right to go.

Saturday, the big day! I surprised Mom by washing up, putting on clean clothes and even combing my hair. The show was great. Harry Langdon, Ben Blue, then a neat western, the Riddle Rider. He could ride into a cave in his black hat and clothes then, instantly, ride right out again in a white outfit, with a mask, so you couldn't tell who he was.

After the show we went to Conyer's Confectionery. She had a root beer float, I had a pineapple, marshmallow nut sundae.

When I took her home we stopped at the gate.

"Can I kiss you?"

She nodded, closed her eyes and puckered up. As our lips touched, all hell broke loose. The door slammed. Looking past her I could see her father coming off the porch, down the steps, yelling at me.

"I'll fix you!"

I turned and ran fast as I could. Looking back I could see those long legs hurdling that white, picket fence.

"I can't outrun those long legs!" I didn't hear him coming or feel his hands, so I looked back. He was stopped, just waving his fist. I ran all the way home.

"What have you been up to, young man?"

"Dad! Mr. Black was going to beat me up. He chased me and yelled at me!"

"Why would he do that?"

"He saw me kissing Ruth! I guess. I ran all the way home. I'm scared!"

"I can see you are. I think he was just joking. Having some fun with you."

"It wasn't funny to me."

"He wouldn't hurt you. He's a nice guy."

I never went back to Ruth's house. A long time later I went into his Drug Store. He didn't notice me.

Wagon

Strange things happen on Halloween. We had been out tipping over outhouses and throwing gravel on the German doctor's metal roof. He would come out and cuss at us in German. Then when we did it again he would switch to English.

The next morning I went to feed Tony and there was a wagon, alongside the barn. It had been pushed down from Leadville Street, hit the barn and stopped. After throwing some hay in the manger, I took a look at the wagon. It was a buckboard. Light weight, with a bed in the back for hauling stuff. It was in real good shape. We just left it there. You could see it from Leadville, also from Main Street. We figured someone would claim it. No one ever did.

I decided that Tony could pull that wagon, so I borrowed a harness from Bill. His dad had a grocery store, sold coal, which was delivered by horse and wagon, or in the winter by sleigh. The buckboard was a single horse rig with shafts, instead of a tongue.

My brother helped me hook Tony to the wagon. Tony didn't want anything to do with this new idea of mine. The only way we could work it was for me to sit on the seat and Clyde would lead Tony. This got old for Tony and my brother, so it took a lot of coaxing of both of them before Tony would pull it by himself.

All this time I was remembering a runaway that I had seen. We had been playing baseball when we heard somebody yelling, "Runaway! Runaway!" I had jumped the fence to the sidewalk on Main Street. Here they came! Two wild, frantic mustangs, pulling a light delivery wagon from Tintic Mercantile. There was no one on the street, so they had a straight run. The wagon was bouncing all around from hitting the chuckholes. All the grocery boxes were flying around in the back. A lot of them were ending up on the road.

A miner jumped out to the middle of the street shouting, "Whoa there! Whoa there!" while waving his arms and his lunch bucket. What he did made the mustangs swerve so that the left rears wheel smacked against a telephone pole. The wheel exploded. The iron rim went hooping down the sidewalk. The last I saw, the wagon was still going like sixty, both back wheels were gone, so the bed was dragging on the road. It looked like a driverless chariot.

I did some thinking about that runaway. I knew that if Tony decided to do that, I'd have a helluva time changing his mind.

Tony, finally, got so he would pull the wagon. I could see he didn't like it. In fact he took any fun out of it in the going away part of the ride. When we headed for home, though, he would really take off and give you a ride.

I finally decided it was a lot easier to use the saddle, so I gave up on the wagon.

That's Life

Tony and I, George and Bob Reynolds chummed around a lot. They didn't have a horse so we would take turns on Tony. They couldn't ride as good as I could, but they were learning. One day we had been out to the Cole Canyon Cliffs and got back to their house at suppertime. They had a big family, five boys and two girls. They were "poor." Their father was a miner, working for the Chief Consolidated Mining Company, and was sick a lot. He had "Rock on the Lung" (Miners consumption) which killed most of the young men who worked in the mines, before they were forty.

One time I found a twenty-dollar bill on the galvanized roofing on our dugout just behind our house. We figured some drunk had wandered off the trail and fell, caving in the roof and had left the bill there I guess, for wrecking our dugout. That was a lot of money in 1926. I gathered Bob and George Reynolds and some other kids, and we went on a candy and soda binge. I sent a five-dollar bill home with George to Mrs. Reynolds cause I knew Mr. Reynolds hadn't worked for several weeks. Just laying around and coughing. She hugged me every time I came around after that.

This day Bob and George insisted on me staying to eat with them. I felt guilty about that, but they asked Mrs. Reynolds. She said, "Of course. We would love to have you."

We all sat down at the table. I was surprised to see Jack, their eldest son there. He had been gone for nearly a year, working here and there.

There wasn't much talk while we all feasted on stew stuff,

then sopped it up with buttered, homemade bread. When Mr. Reynolds got done and was drinking his coffee, between coughing spells, he looked over at Jack. "What happened, why did they lay you off?"

"Well, I just got tired of them raggin' me around. They seemed to know every move I made. I told Shorty about it being a real chicken operation. Later one of the owner's boys, Chad came up to me and said. 'You got a bad attitude, Jack. Seem to think this is some kinda game. We think it's a very serious business and we aim to succeed at it.'"

"I wasn't going to take any of his guff so I said, 'WELL, GOOD FOR YO-U-U!' Just like that."

"Chad looked at me, shifted his cud, spit, and said, 'You're fired! Go pick up your time.' I glared at him, but he just turned and walked away. I told Shorty I'd see him around, went to the office and picked up my check. I figure, who needs an outfit like that?"

"What are you gonna do now?"

"Well, I'll probably check at the Dividend Smelter in a few days. No hurry. Gotta get my feet on the ground again."

"You save any money?"

"Naw, I had some but I got in a crap game a while back. Got wiped out. Never did see such a run of bad luck, but then that's life."

We had all finished supper, and cleaned our plates by then.

Mr. Reynolds stood up. He looked at his wife. Her shoulders slumped, her head dropped, she folded her hands in her lap. He reached across the table, picked up Jack's plate, held it with both hands at the sides, and slammed it down on the edge of the table. It broke in two, clean as a whistle. He chucked it in the garbage, then said, "Yep, that's life! Good luck son!"

Later George told me, "Mom fed him breakfast."

Tony, Honey and Hail

I had taken Tony and rode through Knightsville, over the pass toward Dividend. This was the same area where Dean and I had gotten the honey. Dean had told Mom about a honey tree that he had found. "Could she use some honey?"

"You bet!"

Dean got all rigged up with some netting, gloves, rubber bands for his sleeves and pants legs. He found a tub, rustled up a scoop and an axe. We had walked up the mountain carrying all that stuff. The honey tree was an old hollow snag, but there sure were a lot of bees buzzing around there.

Dean made a smudge fire and smoked the bees for quite a while. It really slowed them down a lot. He took the axe, tub and scoop, then went in after the honey. Dean was fifteen and I was only eight, so I just stood and watched. He came out of the smoke with about three gallons of honey.

When we got home we set the tub down in the yard, then went and got Mom.

"It's all full of dead bees, charcoal, it looks terrible!"

Dean was real disappointed. "Maybe we could strain it," he said.

"See what you can do." Mom said. She went back in the house.

We saved a little, but finally gave up on it.

Tony and I wandered around looking for the tree but never found it. We headed back to town. It had been getting darker and darker. Suddenly we were in one helluva hailstorm. The stones were as big as marbles. I had never seen anything like this and

Tony just went wild with fear. I was really scared. I could barely control Tony, I thought he was going to throw me. I tried to make him gallop toward town, but that just seemed to make the hail worse.

We came to an old abandoned shack. The door was open so I jumped down and pulled Tony into the cabin. This was even worse, cause the hail hitting the roof would drive you deaf. I finally got Tony back outside. He was dancing and whirling so I had a lot of trouble getting back in the saddle.

We finally got back down to Main Street. The hail had stopped, but there was over a foot of water running down the street. Worst flash flood in years. Tony wasn't about to wade it. No way I could get him into it. Our house and barn were on the other side of town.

I was soaking wet by this time, so I tied Tony up to Randall's corral then worked my way down and across to my house. Later, after the storm, I brought Tony to the barn.

Uncle Brig

Uncle Brig would stop at our house on his way back from Salt Lake City. This happened every three or four years. Now he was coming again. I couldn't wait. He had invited me to visit, for two weeks, the last time he had come. I had a wonderful time. He had all kinds of fruit trees and let me try to ride a calf. That was when I was about eight, now I was eleven.

Uncle Brig was a big man, tall and rangy, with wide shoulders, a broad pleasant smile and twinkling eyes to match. He always made you feel like you were somebody special. When I was little, he would put me on his knee and sing about Napoleon.

> I had a horse that I called Napoleon
> All on account of his bony parts
> He was sired by an old Hambletonian
> From that horse I'd never part
>
> He had a frame just like an elephant
> Hair as fine as any silk
> Hitched him to my old milk wagon
> When I'd wanna stop
> I'd holler milk
>
> Slept in a barn last Sunday evening
> All on account of being broke
> Slept in a barn with my mouth wide open
> And a great big rat run down my throat
> I put some cheese upon my teeth

Got a big tomcat full of fleas
Up came the rat and saw the cat
Down went the rat, cat and whole damn cheese.

I went to the fair and I took Napoleon
Entered him in the final race
All the crowd hooted and hollered
"That bag of bones can't stand the pace"

Down the street we went a scootin'
Smiles all over my gosh darned face
Sure as a sinner I was comin' in a winner
When a sucker hollered "MILK!"
And I lost the race.

After he had hugged Mom and Reta, shook hands with Dad and all us boys, we sat around and listened as he told us what he had been doing. He was an expert sheep shearer. He traveled Utah, Wyoming, and Montana doing that. He and Aunt Bec (Rebecca) had a service station and store, too.

Uncle Brig was also a horse trader. He always had the best racehorse in the county. Dad and Mom talked to him half the night.

The next day Uncle Brig said, "Don, I wonder if you could help me out? I've a little mare for Shirley," (Shirley was his boy, about eight), "but I need an experienced horseman to ride her some, before I turn her over to Shirley. Could you come down, for a couple of weeks, and work on that pony?"

I had a great big mixture of scare and thrill. My heart was beating like sixty and my grin must have been as wide as his smile.

"Oh yes! If it's all right with Mom and Dad."

"I've already asked them. It's alright with them."

Mom and I packed my clothes. She told me to behave myself, and then I left with Uncle Brig. I tried to act big, but I did a lot of thinking about how wild this mare was. I couldn't let him know that— not a bit.

"I understand you have been riding a horse for your neighbor's kid?"

"Yeah," I said. "They asked me to ride him some cause Bud couldn't handle him."

"Oh, was he wild?"

"No, just kinda frisky and crazy. He would rear and then go right over backwards."

"When you were riding him?"

"Yup, but Dad fixed that!"

"How'd he do that?"

"When I told Dad the horse went over backwards with me, he said, 'We'll teach him! We'll cure him!'"

"We went down to Dad's garage and into the parts room. Dad got a hunk of three-quarter inch hose a couple of feet long, put a bolt about six inches long in one end, taped it in, then made a cord loop for my wrist. Next he slit the other end of the hose, in several places, about a foot up. I now had a rubber quirt with a bolt in one end."

"Dad said, 'Here's what you do. When he rears up, you switch ends with this and smack him between the ears with the bolt end. Hard!'"

"Really! Did it work?"

"You bet, when I kicked his ribs he started to rare up so I swung that clobber and laid that bolt end in there hard. He shuddered and his head went down between his legs. When his head came back up I kicked again and he went ahead. Only tried it twice."

"Well, I don't think Lady will try any of that."

After all the huggin' and squeezin', from Aunt Bec, and sayin' "HI" to my cousins, I went outside to check over the layout. Three horses were in the corral. For the first few minutes all I could see was the big, red gelding, he called "Blaze," with a strip of white on his face and a powerful red body. This was his special racer. The other two were bays, one being a mare.

The next morning, after breakfast, Uncle Brig took me out to the corral. We saddled "Lady." She was skittish, so he helped me on her. She danced around some, but didn't buck or do any wild stuff.

"You all right?"

"Oh! Sure, she's just fine."

I rode her around the yard and worked with her. She was not hard to handle. Next day I took her for a ride around town. I met a kid named Frank, who had a horse, so we teamed up. After a few days, Frank and I chased deer and checked out the country.

I was at Uncle Brig's for two weeks, then had to go home. He thanked me for "breaking" Lady. He sure knew how to make me feel good.

I didn't tell him about the exciting ride on Lady. It was on the first bareback ride. I went out to Frank's farm. I had made a quirt out of quarter inch rope. I doubled it, then tied a knot, so I had a loop for my wrist. I then tied another knot about eight inches back from the double end.

At Frank's farm the gate was a couple hundred yards from the house. The lane was fenced on both sides. You had to get down, open the gate, go through, close the gate and get back on the horse.

After Frank and I had jawed some, I got back on Lady and headed out. I decided to gallop to the gate so swung the quirt and took off. What happened was that the quirt went under her tail, she clamped down on it and the knot kept me from pulling it out.

She was running like hell. I couldn't get my hand out of the loop, couldn't pull the quirt out, couldn't stop her and couldn't fall off. I had one wild ride to the gate.

She stopped at the gate, whirled and danced, but I was able to slip off, grab the reins, then get the rope out and heave it over the fence. The rest of the ride home was quieter.

Tony – Always a Rebel

One time a buddy of Deans wanted Tony for a deer hunt. I said OK. So they saddled him up. The guy took off. It didn't last long. He was back in a few minutes, leading Tony.

He was galloping up Leadville Street, when Tony ducked into an alley. The saddle slipped under Tony's belly and the guy went flying to the gravel. They should have punched Tony in the belly when they tightened the cinch.

Another time my sister, Reta, was galloping up Leadville, going to visit a friend. She had both hands on the horn. The reins were slack so Tony did a quick 90-degree turn to the right, headed for the barn. He was going so fast, it was all down hill, so he couldn't stop before he got to Main Street. Reta was hanging onto the horn and screaming all the way. One thing, she stayed on the horse.

I had this girlfriend, Taffy. She wanted to borrow Tony. I saddled him up, helped her on and she got on her way. She didn't know anything about horses. For some reason, Tony behaved. She rode him all the way to Knightsville, then got off to visit a friend.

A couple of hours later, my brother found me and said that I had to go and get Tony. He wouldn't let Taffy near him to get back on. She was scared spitless, so just left him there.

I tried a lot of things with Tony. Made a polo mallet, went to our baseball field to try it out. The field had no grass, so was rough and had lots of rocks on it. I tried to hit a baseball. I was using the mallet like a hammer, with head end instead of sideways, like polo players do. I would gallop by the ball and swing mightily. Missed every time. I swung under Tony's neck one time, nearly tripped him, and so gave up on Polo.

I tried some cowboy stuff, too. I liked the way Tom Mix would grab the horn with both hands, pull his legs up into a tuck. His Tony would break into a gallop. When they were going real good, Tom would drop his feet to the ground, his body would fly straight out, and he'd wind up in the saddle. My Tony stopped when my feet hit the ground. I must have tumbled fifty feet.

Another stunt was to run and put your hands on the horse's rump and vault onto his back. Tony wouldn't stand still for that either. He would move just as my hands touched him, so I would wind up with a sudden course change, and pick myself out of the dirt again.

During the winters, Tony mostly got fat and grew long hair. Dad got some cork shoes with some sharp nails sticking out of the bottom, so he wouldn't slip on the ice. We would ski with a guy in the saddle and a towrope around the horn. It wasn't really as much fun as skiing down the mine dumps or on the hills. We gave it up.

I never had any broken bones so, you might say, I was the winner.

Tony – The End

Dad started talking about selling the Garage and the Service Station so he could buy a ranch. I was the happiest kid in town. I'd dream about Tony and me on a nice ranch, with cattle, and a remuda (more horses). My brothers and I, and, of course, Dad, could easy handle a good-sized ranch. There would be five of us, with Dad. He looked around some but never, really, found "THE RANCH."

Next thing you know the Stock Market crashed. It wasn't long before Dad told us that he was going to lose all his property, except the house. I heard Mom and Dad talking, at night. They were some worried, not just about the money, but us boys. Dad said, "My boys are not going in the mines. I worked in them for years. They are no place for our young men. (I guess that included me, even though I was only thirteen.)

They finally decided to move to Salt Lake City. Dad sold the house and whatever else he could. I heard Dad say that he could have saved everything if he had the $1500 he had paid for the National Cash Register. It was the latest thing, helped keep the books.

Course, I had to get rid of Tony. Couldn't take him to Salt Lake City. A guy from the valley bought Tony for seven dollars, and took him away. I never got over that. Good old Tony.

We moved to Salt Lake City, then to Berkeley, California. When I graduated from High School, I went back home for a visit before going to Alaska. Some of my friends told me they saw Tony running in the hills, after I left. I guess he broke loose and went back to his old stomping grounds. I know it's not possible, but I like to think of old Tony, still roaming around Dry Valley, Cole Canyon Cliffs, the Aspen Grove and the Wild Horse Corral.

The Smell of the Yukon

"Did you ever hear of "The Spell of the Yukon?"

"Sure, a great poem by Robert Service."

"Well, I'm going to write about the 'The Smell of the Yukon!'"

Yah see, my dad, brother and I were part of, over 200 people, jammed in the hold, traveling steerage class, on the Alaska Steamship Yukon," Seattle to Seward, April 1935. Steerage meant that you were confined to the hold, or the foredeck. You were prohibited from going above deck or mingling with the regular passengers.

We were there, after six months of saving and planning by the entire family of seven. We were going to make a new start in a new land. The stock market crash of "Twenty Nine" and the "Depression" had changed our lives. Dad had been a very successful car dealer in Eureka, Utah when the crash wiped him out. He was determined that his four boys would not go in the mines and die young. He moved us to Salt Lake City and eventually to Berkeley, California, our take off point for the Alaskan Adventure.

I was in high school, selling newspapers on a street corner before school, and banking my 50 cents a day. Dean, my brother, worked at the Ford plant, in Richmond, and Dad was selling vacuum cleaners. Everyone was working and contributing.

We bought a seven by nine-foot tent and pitched it in the living room of our flat. This was to be our home in Alaska. As a gag I bought a corncob pipe and some Raleigh tobacco, lit up and sat in front of the tent. I was testing my Dad to see what he would do about it. I was not interested in smoking as I spent my spare time in boxing, tumbling and basketball. Dad never said a word. This stupid stunt started a habit that lasted for forty years.

There was a bus war on at the time, so we traveled from Oakland to Seattle for ten dollars apiece. Arriving in Seattle we boarded the Yukon. The fare to Seward was forty dollars each, steerage class. We were led into the hold of the ship and assigned a berth. This consisted of a canvas stretcher with two by four wooden sides, which were lashed to upright four by four posts with stringy, sisal rope. They were seven berths high and the spacing had been based on the size of the majority of the passengers. They were small, Filipino, cannery workers, so we larger types could not roll over in our bunks. Our meals were scrambled eggs for breakfast, canned meat and beans with boiled potatoes with the jackets on. Every day the same diet. Almost caused a riot. The dining area was off limits. There were no tables or chairs, lounge area, or any other amenities to ease the passage.

In severe weather, such as the crossing of the Gulf of Alaska, the lashings on the bunks could fail and did. One Norwegian, on the top bunk had that happen to him. He landed on his back in the aisle. "I be a lop-sided Christ!" was his expletive, as he picked himself off the deck.

The Gulf of Alaska is a very shallow bay, subject to extremely rough seas. That's what we hit on the sixth day out of Seattle. Sickness curbed the spirit of mutiny. Our hold, with at least 100 sick souls, was an incredible miasma of misery. Many could not leave their bunks for relief, so soiled their space with vomit and body waste. Attendants were not on hand to rectify the problems. There was no escape from the stench for any length of time. The lingering aroma of previous cargo, such as cattle, spoiled vegetables and fruit blended with errant traces of oil, fish, solvents and boiled potatoes. Two hundred sick, unwashed, would be pioneers added a final bouquet to the stench. That was when I first heard the expression. "That would gag a maggot!"

The only relief, for the able, was to escape to the fresh air and stormy area of the foredeck. Others and I stood there for hours. If you got cold and tired enough, you could get to sleep, on your bunk, before getting sick.

No one died, that I know of. The arrival in Seward proved a welcome rebirth of hope and spirit to all of us. I was following the line to the gangplank, to disembark, when I looked down. There on the deck, at my feet, was a beautiful twenty-dollar bill. I quickly rescued it from the future grasp of some unworthy soul. Now our trio had the magnificent sum of $120.00 between us.

We docked in Seward on April 5, 1935 and everyone went their separate ways to fame, fortune or failure. We, three, boarded the train to Anchorage. We were some of the lucky ones who prospered.

In 1935 the United States was still in the Great Depression. There were few jobs and survival was a struggle for most people. It took me six months to save the required $50.00 for my fare from Oakland to Seward, Alaska. Most of the passengers were Filipinos who would work in the fish canneries for the season. The others were searching for the better life they might find on the "Last Frontier." Our voyage was nasty, but short. My friends, Duke and Ed Jurgeliet, laid off machinists from Detroit, headed for Alaska, but arrived in Seattle with no more money. Their solution was to hitchhike and walk from Seattle to Haines, Alaska. Quite a feat when you consider there was no road most of the way. Duke figured they traveled about two thousand miles. They would work when they could, living off the land by killing game and fishing. Also, panned a little gold. It took two years, but they made it.

Anchorage

We arrived in Anchorage on April 5, 1935. There were three or four inches of snow, but it wasn't very cold. Anchorage had about 2500 people, one main street, several bars and restaurants, and a thriving Red Light District on the East End. Everyone we met was friendly and helpful.

Before leaving California we had read of the Government's plan to colonize the Matanuska Valley. Two hundred families from the Midwest were to be given forty acres of land, together with a house, equipment, livestock, a truck, etc. A total of twenty thousand dollars credit, per family. The plan was to create a farm industry to supply Anchorage and the "Railbelt," Seward to Fairbanks. Our hope was to be a part of this endeavor.

While investigating this project, and also the possibility of homesteading, we visited the Bureau of Land Management office. While there we met Mr. Felton, who was Postmaster, at what would become Palmer in the Matanuska Valley. He told us that the first colonists would arrive in about two weeks and there would be jobs available constructing facilities to be used by them on their arrival. He invited us to pitch our tent in his yard until we could get settled.

There wasn't much to do while waiting for the next train to Palmer. The highway had not been constructed yet, so we wandered around town. Passing Seidenverg's Clothing Store we stopped in to kill time and look around. Mr. Seidenverg greeted us and asked us our plans. He knew at a glance that we were Chechakos.

When we told him our plans to go to Palmer to find work, he asked us what kind of clothes we had. We learned, at once, that we were not outfitted for the kind of work we would be doing. Shoepacs, rain gear, Tin Pants, woolen underwear, mosquito nets, etc. Dad said," We have no money for all that stuff!" Mr. Seidenverg shrugged, then said, "No problem, I will help you pick out what you will need and you can pay me in the fall." After five years of bare survival in the depression-ridden States of Utah and California, we could not believe that such an act of faith was possible. We left with the full wardrobe necessary to survive in this new land.

Palmer was nothing more than a shack for a railroad station and store, owned by Mr. Felton. We three were the only ones who got off the train. There were twelve or fifteen people surrounding Mr. Felton. The conductor gave him a bag of mail. Everyone followed him into the building where he sorted the mail. Most of it was handed out to the lucky ones. Within moments everyone was gone but Mr. Felton and the three of us. They just seemed to vanish.

Three adults, living in a 7x9-foot tent, cooking on a little sheet metal, Yukon stove, eating beans, rice, stew and sourdough bread. That was our lot in life for the first few weeks. The bread was a remnant of Dad's life as a sheepherder, thirty-five years before. He had bragged of his expertise, but somehow it had waned. The only way we could possible eat the loaves was to attack them as soon as they came out of the oven. If they were allowed to cool, there was no way you could cut, break or bite the stuff.

Our first jobs were for the "Corporation" which was the agency that managed the colony project. We built tent frames, dug outhouse holes and other chores in preparation for the first arrivals. With money coming in, our diet improved. Store bought bread on occasion and, I'll never forget, a large can of peaches!

Another squatter in Mr. Felton's yard was the Reverend B. J. Bingle. With his wife and two children he was living in two tents while a house was being built for them. They were a fine family. He would save many souls in the future, I was sure.

The colonists arrived. Many got off with rifles, ready for the great Alaskan wilderness. Others got off with gold pans. They were housed in tents and in a few days there was a drawing where each was given a description of the location of their forty-acre parcel. Some, fortunate ones, received cleared land while the others got only solid birch, alder and spruce forest land. All the access roads were not in yet so many were, immediately, discouraged and ready to return home.

We, of course, could not get in on this colonist thing, so were investigating the availability of homestead land. We learned of an open area between Bodenburg Butte and the Knik River, about seven miles from Palmer. We left Palmer and walked the gravel road to the Matanuska River. Crossing the new bridge we entered the uncleared right-of-way. The trees had been fallen and hauled to the edge, but all the stumps, and brush, were still standing. Following the right-of-way we encountered two different, bachelor Homesteaders and stopped in to say hello and have a cup of coffee. One was using a hand turned windlass to pull the stumps. We helped turn the lever as far as we could. He had used this primitive method to pull several stumps and had then planted potatoes and other vegetables in the ten or twelve foot circle of soil thus exposed. My thought was, "My God, clearing forty acres would take forever."

We left the right-of-way after passing the Butte. We attempted to find the land we thought was open. We found none of the references we had been told to look for and as night fell we prepared to "Siwash" it overnight. Siwash is a native Alaskan term for camping with no food or gear. We built a small fire under a large spruce tree, made some swamp water tea, and huddled, under the branches, for the several hours 'til dawn. We were in a swampy area so the rain and the necessary headnets, to ward of the multitude of mosquitoes, made a miserable ordeal.

Daybreak, visible mountains, a choice of directions, and we were on our way to civilization, we hoped. Breaking out onto the right of way we saw a cluster of tents, to one side. Mr. Nelson, the only person there, greeted us warmly and invited us into, what became evident, a mess tent. We learned that Mr. Nelson was the foreman of the Road Commission crew. He had spent the winter as caretaker of the camp. They would be hiring a crew shortly for the season's work. We were welcome company for him. He offered to cook breakfast for us. When Nelson opened the door to the storage area, I couldn't believe my eyes. The goddamn room was full of food. Instantly I thought, "I'm going to work for this outfit! That's as near to heaven as I'll ever get!" I told myself. We enjoyed an unforgettable meal of canned peaches, ham, eggs, and hotcakes, all washed down with buckets of good coffee. A-A-A-H!

The three of us went to work on a survey crew, slashing lines for the 40-acre parcels. In June I cut my foot badly with an ax and was laid up for a month.

In the meantime Dean came up from Berkeley to join us. He had written, asking about wild game, especially moose. We wrote back and told him we had seen no moose but we had seen tracks.

"You can't eat tracks!" was his terse reply.

When he arrived he couldn't wait to go hunting. We were working, so he went alone early one morning. After work and even after dinner he still hadn't returned. Finally he showed up an exhausted, nervous wreck. Mosquitoes buzzing all around him in spite of this frantic waving and slapping at them. We are listening to his story and calmly waiting until a mosquito had settled on our hands or face and then, unhurriedly wiping it into oblivion.

"My God!— I couldn't get away from them. I even climbed, way up in a tree. They followed me up there! How can you stand it?"

"Oh! You just get used to them."

Dean and I went to work for the Road Commission. We were slashing right of way, carrying corduroy logs, and digging ditches alongside to cover them up.

Our boss, Tom McCrea, was a rough talking Canadian, 70-year-old ex-logger. One day a guy showed up in camp. He was dressed in a white shirt, slacks and low cut shoes. He had jumped ship in Seward. Although he was a cook, Tom hired him as regular crew.

About a week later, at dinner, Tom was grumbling about the fact that the ex-cook had left without saying a word to anyone. "I didn't mind the son of a bitch leaving, but he took my new boots."

"Were those your boots?" Dean asked. "Well they weren't any good anyway."

"What the hell do you mean, they weren't any good? Tom yelled. "They were twenty dollar, brand new cork boots!"

"I was working with him," Dean said. "He complained that the boots were hurting his Achilles tendon, so he took them off, laid them on a stump and, with his ax, cut a slash in the back at the troublesome spot."

" That dirty bluenosed son of a bitch. I'll kill that bastard!" Looking at me he said, "Can you drive a truck, Kid!"

I nodded.

"Come on, I'll get him if I have to look all week!"

We drove all over the valley, but never found a trace of the bluenose.

What Dean didn't tell Tom was that it was at Dean's suggestion that the cook cut the boots.

Bud

I grin every time I think of Ol' Bud. In '35 Bud was in his early seventies. I was eighteen. He was foreman on the Alaska Territorial Road Commission; I was one of his truck drivers. We were graveling the road from the Matanuska River, just out of Palmer, ten or eleven miles away. Our camp was near Bodenburg Butte. In fact, we were taking gravel from the Butte.

Bud Whitney was a small man, probably five feet six and weighed, maybe, one hundred twenty-five pounds. Ramrod straight, he had all his hair (white) and all his teeth. He credited the latter to daily brushing with Arm and Hammer Baking Soda. Bud wore a Canadian Mountie Stetson hat, and was always neat and clean. Which was not easy in a tent camp over a five to seven month season.

By the winter of '35, we were hauling gravel to the Knik River where they were building a bridge. Another crew was at mile 146, on the railroad, building road from Anchorage to the Knik River, so that when the bridge was completed, you would be able to drive from Anchorage clear to Palmer, all of fifty miles.

Bud and his wife Daisy had homesteaded just north of what is now Anchorage in 1912. The year 1914 saw the U. S. Government come in, lay out the townsite, auction the lots and build the Alaska Railroad yard and roundhouse. It was to service the railroad, which was under construction. The railroad would link the city of Seward with Fairbanks, four hundred miles away in the interior of Alaska.

When prohibition came to the country in 1918, Bud didn't believe in the law, so had a fairly prosperous life as a bootlegger 'til 1932 when the law was repealed.

By November our main job was to furnish the gravel and cement to the crew building the Knik River Bridge. They had built a false bridge out of timber, had sunken caissons through the ice, dug down to bedrock and were forming and pouring the concrete piers, in the steam heated caissons. The piers would support the steel structure of the bridge. Our job was to back our trucks from the bank, over the wooden false bridge, to the pier location, delivering gravel and cement. Because it was the only winter work available, to the Road Commission personnel, the crew was mainly foremen and superintendents, from all over the Territory.

At first we, the young truck drivers, had a lot of fun. Whenever we had a work break, we would take the trucks down on the river ice. We would go on the sandbar, then come charging back as fast as those old trucks would ramble, run out on the ice, slam on the brakes and spin the steering wheel. Because the ice was slick and smooth we could spin, round and round for a couple of hundred yards. Soon we would have the whole bridge-work gang, standing there watching us. Another time we had to take the trucks to the far side of the river to bring back supplies. We each had a laborer to help load the cargo. Cliff had a Dutchman, maybe sixty-five years old, who was deathly afraid of the icy river. Cliff would jam the throttle down, spin the wheels and come to a complete stop. Old Dutch would get out of the truck and start walking. After he had walked a hundred yards, or so, Cliff would ease in the clutch and move out. When he got to the Dutchman he would stop and ask him to get in. Then he would spin out trying to get moving again. Dutchy would get out and start to walk. Cliff worked this so the Dutchman walked most of the mile to the other bank. Oh well! God may punish him.

We lived in large, six man tents with a big barrel stove in the center. Six different personalities, depressing darkness, constant cold, two glaring gasoline lanterns, with no recreation or radio. We read or shot the bull. This led to complications in our relations with the other workers.

"Midnight John" was the powder monkey's helper. They drilled the holes into the frozen face of the gravel pit, tamped in the dynamite and then blasted the gravel to the floor of the pit. The power shovel could then load our trucks and we would gravel the roads or deliver to the bridge for the concrete piers.

Eli Boravich was a Russian refugee, now a laborer on our gang. He and the Dutchman would, using number two shovels, throw the bigger rocks off the road when we dumped the load. You could not call it gravel. It was what they called "pit run." Any thing over six inches though was tossed into the borrow pit.

The first time I saw Eli he was sitting on the edge of his cot, getting ready for bed. He pulled his right leg out of his pants, then instead of pulling his left out, just reached down and set his leg, pants and all, aside then laid it on a shelf.

Eli hated Midnight John. The other gravel spreader, the Dutchman, shared this hatred. When these two old immigrants started to recite to each other John's shortcomings they became both hysterical and unintelligible.

It was Midnight John's regimen to sack out, after dinner, for two or three hours. He would wake up, then, about ten o'clock. This, of course, was bedtime for the other tentmates and especially Eli and his partner. John would proceed to shave, brush his teeth, wash and comb his hair, stare at himself in the mirror to detect any possible blemish, stray whisker, etc. All this time, of course, the gas lantern was on and its brilliant, white glare was hard to escape, especially for the two old guys, as they were the nearest to it. There was a lot of grumbling, but no direct action until...

Eli and Dutch had washed up and were waiting for the dinner gong. Both were tired and miserable from a long, cold, day of shoveling rocks. They started grumbling about John. We others, spurred them on until when John finally appeared through the tent flap, he was confronted by two irate, incoherent, shouting old men. Bewildered, he ducked back out and only returned after dinner. Eli, Dutch and John followed the same sleep schedule from then on.

John was also very fastidious about his bunk and area. He had a brand new Woods Arctic Eiderdown Sleeping Bag. That was the very best bag you could buy. Cost a month's wages. He would spend several minutes fluffing it up and smoothing it out before he left for work. No wrinkles on John's bed.

The road grader operator was John's exact opposite. He would go for weeks without changing his clothes or shaving. One day the grader guy came through on his run. While there, he decided to change oil on his machine. He crawled under the grader, took out the oil plug and drained on the ground. When it quit running he went back under and, lying in the oil pool, replaced the plug. After putting the new oil in he decided to take a short rest. He dropped into our tent, and flopped on the first cot. John's of course. Tragedy! He left before John returned. Good thing, I think gentle John would have killed him.

It was cold. Sometimes going down as far as 40 below zero. We had no alcohol to put in the radiators of the trucks. This was before the modern anti-freeze products like Prestone etc. To keep the trucks from freezing up the bull cook would keep them running all night, a miserable, cold job. He was also charged with keeping the fires in the tents stoked all night. He would wake us up in the morning by coming into the tent with a small can of gasoline. He would swing the door of the barrel stove open and shout. "You sons a bitches shaved yet?" Then he would toss the can of gas into the stove. The explosion would light up the tent and flames would shoot out the stove door clear to the entrance flap. In seconds we were standing and when our nerves settled we would start to get our clothes on. Irv, the cowboy, would of course, grab for his Stetson first.

The Road Commission was always short of money— no such thing as overtime or benefits. You worked seven days a week, with only two holidays, the Fourth of July and Christmas. To save money the bridge crew did not spike the bridge decking (4 by 12's, twenty two feet long), to the stringers. So when you varied from the exact center, while backing out to the pier, the ends of the planks would raise and lower in a wave as you progressed toward the pier. This was hazardous. Another complication was that, in late January and February, we were backing on, icy planking, in darkness against the headlights of the off-coming trucks. You had to stand on the running board, one foot on the gas pedal, and one hand on the steering wheel, head craned to see where the hell you were. This could go on for a quarter of a mile. The only place the trucks could pass was at the piers. I don't remember worrying about it, it was just something you did, your job. Bud, though, was worried about us and tried to get the crew to improve things. At least nail down the decking. They said, "No dice." Bud got to drinking, not shaving and was brooding.

One day I backed on with a full load of sacked cement. You had to back just right to get in along side the hopper, to unload the cement. The edge of the bridge was on my blind side and I cut too soon, so that before they got me stopped, I had the outside dual and half of the inside wheel hanging with nothing under it but the river ice twenty-five feet below. Bud was there and he was furious.

A few minutes later, Cliff backed up on the hopper ramp with a load of gravel, broke through the ramp and the truck crashed to the main deck. Bud saw this, too, and exploded.

"You guys go back to camp and stay there! Tell the others!"

Bud shut down the whole operation, told the bridge guys to make the bridge safe to work on or he would send his crew to town. Being the lowest ranking authority on the project, he laid it all on the line.

We hung around camp for a couple of days, Bud was unshaven, half drunk, worried about losing his much needed job. Not talking. We were all sure he would be fired, but the brass improved the conditions, as directed, and we all went back to work. We poured the last pier in February of '36.

The Knik Glacier is just a few miles from the bridge. The wind would come off the ice; the temperature would drop to forty below zero. One time the wind was so strong that it blew the 18-ton pile driver off the bridge. The pile driver was on greased skids, so it could be moved more easily with the winch. The wind sailed it off and scattered it for a quarter mile down the sand bar. The steel structure, sitting on the false bridge was within one I-beam of reaching the next pier. That span was knocked five feet out of line, so required that a Bulldozer, with a winch, be anchored upriver, a line run to the end of the steel structure, the span be hauled back in line.

"Cement Pete" held down the worst job I have ever seen. Pete's job was to rip open the sacks of cement, and dump them into the hopper. He had to face the glacier wind, so probably inhaled a half sack of cement a week. His face, hair, eyes and clothes were solid cement at the end of eight hours.

We were living in tents, with a barrel stove, which had a five gallon gas can of water warming on it. No shower, except in Palmer, where we went every week or so. Pete survived the job, but I don't know how much longer.

We had six weeks where we never saw the sun. The Knik River Bridge is right under Pioneer Peak, 7500 feet high, so as the sun wanders around the horizon, in Alaska, in the winter, it never got high enough to clear the peak. One day it appeared for a few seconds in a blinding flash, then, day by day, the brightness lasted longer.

The next summer I went to work for Bud again. We were graveling the roads to the colonist's homes around the Butte.

One day a brand new Gallion road grader was delivered to

our camp. I wanted to run that thing in the worst way. Not one of the crew seemed to know who was to operate it. I walked up to Bud, "Who's the boss around here?" I said.

He looked at me kinda funny, then said, "I don't know!"

"Well, if you see him, tell him that I am the best damn grader operator around!"

Later on, a bunch of us were standing around checking it out, when Bud said to me, "Let's see what you can do!" I hopped on the grader, studied a bit, got it started and in gear. I spun the wheels to lower the blade and started across the yard. I was in hog heaven and not paying attention, so buried the blade in the ground, after digging a swath across the yard. The motor stalled. There I was an abject failure, suffering humiliation and crude remarks from my "friends."

Bud just turned around and walked away. I started her up and worked for a couple of hours repairing the damage to the yard. I was the grader operator for the rest of the season.

Hatcher Pass Sixty Years Later

My wife, Bobbie, and I recently drove the road from Wasilla to Willow. Sixty years ago our crew was extending the road from the Lucky Shot Mine to Willow. The drive brought back vivid memories of the life I lived then.

The road had already been slashed and graded, so our job was to provide the gravel and grade it to a suitable condition, with no rock crusher. The gravel was pit run and was sized from sand to rocks and boulders. We had shovel operators, (#2 hand shovels) who threw anything over 4 inches over the borrow pit into the woods. When the road was driveable (you didn't get stuck), it was considered a finished road.

We lived in tents, five to seven men in each. I was a dump truck driver, 19 years old and happy to be making $4.00 a day plus board and room. Room was a tent.

Wasilla, the supply point for the Willow Creek mining district was on the railroad. The village consisted of Hernings Store, the Cadwalladers Roadhouse, a Community Hall and sixty or so houses.

We lived the past as we drove up along the Little Susitna River to the Museum at the Old Independence mine. Fifty-seven years ago, on our honeymoon we had gone up this road in the dead of winter. February 5, 1941 we had braved the eight foot high snow drifts on each side of the road, in 20 below weather to go up to the Independence Mine, just for a ride. On the way back down we stopped at the Roadhouse. There were several miners killing time at the bar. They quickly guessed we were newlyweds so bought several rounds of hot buttered rum drinks for us. We finally left, happily flying down the snow chute to the valley. Made it just fine.

The road, some better but no highway, carried me back to 1937 for the mountains and streams were unchanged. Light green, dark green, tree lined streams, rocky outcrops, all replayed the vistas of long ago. We stopped at the Independence Mine and Museum, enjoyed the relics, mementos of its past glory. I remembered that this mine was not an important player in the scenes of my time. It's fame and glory came later.

We took the narrow, rutted road from the turnoff, which would lead us to Hatcher Pass. The improvement of this road (trail) had been minimal. Maybe a little wider in spots and some of the more treacherous switchbacks had been improved, but not by much. Pucker passing still occurred between wide spots. The final switchback, now more reasonable, had been a devil to negotiate for our supply driver, Fred Dobler, a veteran of World War I. He had the affliction known as Shell Shock. He was extremely nervous and jumpy. Driving the supply truck heavily loaded with long bridge timbers, he would start around the final switchback only to discover that it was so sharp and steep that the front wheels would leave the ground, thus he had no control of the vehicle. After two or three attempts, he walked the several miles to our camp. Jumping and waving his arms he relived his terrifying trials to the guffaws of an unsympathetic audience. Several of the crew drove back to the trouble spot, stood on the front bumper, others sat on the hood of the truck and they were able to get around the switchback and to the crest of the pass.

Bobbie and I stopped at Summit Lake, a small but beautiful scene to behold. From here you could see where the old road had been abandoned for a distance. The new route was less treacherous than the old. We passed the only active mine in the area, still finding gold. At the bottom of the mountain we stopped for a picnic. Farther down the road we came to the site of the old Lucky Shot Mine, the most successful mine in the

Willow Creek district.

I recalled the cable line, which had carried the ore buckets from the mine, high on the mountain, to the mill at the creek side in the valley. I thought of the miners climbing to the mine from their quarters by the creek and thought that just getting up there would be a day's work. Tough dudes indeed. We could see the thousands of tons of tailings in the mine dump, streaming down to the valley. When you realized that all that rock had been blasted loose, shoveled by hand and transported by the little ore cars to the adit and dumped as waste, the image is overwhelming.

There were over fifty mines in the Willow Creek district. In my time the Gold Cord and the Lucky Shot were the most successful. All were supplied by horse and wagon, and later by trucks from Wasilla or by tractor from the railroad station at Willow. The extension of the road to Willow would simplify supply to these mines.

Lucky Shot employed about 100 men at the time, with 40 or so being miners. There were good accommodations for the men. At Kellyville, a mile or so away, there was a small store, a few cabins and a lovely 18 year old girl named Evelyn. She was a far more beautiful sight than the mountains.

My most notable remembrance of the Lucky Shot was watching a four five six game where, within twenty minutes a miner, who had not gone to town in over a year and a half, lost his stake of over $1100. That was a lesson I retained.

Our crew lived in a tent camp four miles beyond Kellyville. We had five yard dump trucks, a power shovel to load them, a grader, a mechanic with a tent shop, a big cook tent with an excellent cook and a bull cook.

Our foreman was an ex-artillery man from World War I. His mind was still in France I guess, cause he tried to run our operation with military precision. This was not very successful and soon created a lot of resentment. In fact, egged on by the shovel operator, who claimed he had influence with the head guys, we decided to revolt. Somebody had to go, him or us. We had a meeting, and Pansy Karlovich and I were selected to go over to Palmer and present our demands to the Superintendent, Mr. Carl Johnson. Pansy was one tough dude, how he got that name I have no idea because in hockey or baseball he was outstanding. I was just in the revolt for the excitement.

We approached the Superintendent, told our story and awaited his response.

"If you don't like your job, quit! I didn't hire him and I can't fire him!"

We were stunned. This wasn't the way it should go! No job! God!

Carl, half smiling said, "Hold off for a few days."

We left feeling deep, deep failure and disgust.

Carl came over a couple of days later. After his meeting with the Forman, the Forman called us all together and apologized. After that he had no authority at all. His orders were ignored. The crew did the work as they felt if should be done. He got mad at 18-year-old Pete Snyder and fired him. Pete told him he wasn't leaving 'til school started in five weeks. The boy was not easily intimidated. Fact was he had chased a bear out of the cook shack by banging it on the butt with a frying pan. Pete stayed.

When our work moved to the upper valley we were in the land of the beavers. Their dams threatened the road in some places. Blasting them was ineffective, as they would be repaired overnight. The dam's cool inviting appearance was a tempting invitation for escape from the hot dusty cab of my truck. I hid the truck, stripped and made a running dive into one of the beauties. G-A-A-S-P. It was so cold I planed the surface back to the bank. Must have been 33 degrees. Cooled me off, sure nuff!

The road opened excellent moose habitat to the hunters, so when moose season opened we would see and hear the mighty nimrods go by on their safaris. Jack Scott, our grader operator had gotten his moose. He took the head and antlers and wired it to a tree trunk about 70 yards down the road. We would hear a car go by, then Bam! Bam! Bam! It sounded like a small war, then silence. Within a week the head fell out of the tree and silence resumed.

Another time we were driving to Willow after shift and came upon four male nurses from the Palmer Hospital. They surrounded a big old Bull Moose, which was trying to get to its feet in the middle of the road. They had apparently shot it but for some, incomprehensible reasons were not finishing it off. The moose could not get all four feet under him. Jack took his rifle, killed the moose and we were on our way talking about what would have happened to those guys if that sucker had gotten all four feet under him. When we returned we saw the damnest job of butchering we had ever witnessed. Instead of quartering the animal they were piecemeal separating parts and had a canoe frame of bare, shiny ribs left to dispose of. I would have hated to go to their hospital for care.

One of our crew, Jimmy Minano had his own 8x10 tent, and a battery operated radio. He asked me if I would move in with him. So, from then on I enjoyed the music from the Coconut Grove Orchestra in Los Angeles on Saturday nights. By some fluke of nature the reception in our little valley was perfect even though the radio was not short wave. Another real treat was blueberry pie. We had a great cook, Fred Rutledge, who liked to please the crew with special treats. He had a Swedish berry picker and would go out in the berry patches and come back with a whole bucket full of blueberries. His pies were incredibly delicious. I still eat lots of blueberries after he introduced them to me.

One evening I noticed a straight line of brush running for over a mile on the hillside opposite our camp. My curiosity aroused, I crossed the creek, skirted the beaver dams and climbed up to where the line was. It was a ditch about two feet wide and just as deep. I followed it for half a mile where it turned into a draw. Further on I saw the remains of a dam. A miner to bring water to his placer mining site had dug the ditch. Going back I could see that a good part of it was through solid rock. He had blasted where necessary, but had hand dug the ditch the whole distance. The other end turned and went down to the bench by the creek. This was where he had employed a Giant (water nozzle) to move the dirt through sluice boxes to recover the gold, if any. He must have spent years ditching but there was no way to measure his success in finding the gold, if any. I do hope he got rich. Now we saw that line of willows proved that the ditch was still there.

Further on down the valley we saw the old bridge, now replaced by a new and better one. The bridge had memories for me. I had been approaching it at a pretty high speed, carrying a load of gravel, when the tie rod on the steering broke just as I was turning onto the bridge. A couple of stout spruce trees stopped the truck, from going all the way into the creek. Beyond the bridge, my memories of that part of my life ended.

Conover's Cafe
Between Third and Fourth Ave
Anchorage, 1937

I learned of my sister's misapprehension as to the origin of Conover's Cafe after most of the relevant witnesses had passed to the great dining room in the sky. As I was the entrepreneur, (had the bucks) my memory is relatively clear. In the fall of 1937 I came back to Anchorage (having spent seven months in the interior building roads) with over a thousand bucks and no plans. My brother, Clyde had no bucks, but big plans.

My Dad had leased the Morrison Hotel and was managing it. There was a large, unused room on the alley end of the building, measuring about eighteen by forty feet. Clyde came to me and said that we should put a cafe in that unused room. He said that the Cheechako Tavern was remodeling and we could buy seven nice cedar booths for a hundred bucks.

Clyde was a real promoter. He promoted me right into the restaurant business. We were partners, he furnished the ideas, and I furnished the money. We bought a big Lang restaurant range, a refrigerator, sinks, lighting, juke box, dishes, utensils, everything we needed. When I ran out of money I signed the contracts.

Clyde's next contribution was to hire Mac McCarthy, a sixty-something year old camp cook. Mac had been cooking and drinking around Alaska for forty years. He has a host of friends, which was a factor in the immediate high volume of our business.

The food was wonderful and at 75 cents for a full course dinner, soup, salad, roast beef, potatoes and gravy, vegetables plus dessert we had all the business we could handle. Mac also introduced his famous Swedish rye bread. That drew even more customers. We obtained a wine license, and started a radio program advertising dining and dancing. We had room for two couples maybe, but it brought in the people.

My mother, an experienced cook, had been warning me about the size of the portions Mac was dishing out to his friends. It seemed like everyone was his friend. Mom said we were losing money on every plateful! Dad then stepped in, with his experienced business eye. He soon discerned that we were in deep trouble financially. We suddenly became me. Clyde lost interest in the hard work connected with the cafe and pulled away to pursue other avenues for his talents.

I couldn't leave. I was the one who owed the money! I got rid of Mac. Mom came in as cook. We struggled through the winter of 38-39, working 14 to 16 hour shifts with no time off and no money to spend. By April we had the debt down to seven hundred dollars.

The Territorial Road Commission had contacted me again about working for them. I told Mom I would go back to road building, and would come back in six or seven months with over a thousand dollars. I told her I was going to pay off the debt and then she could have the business.

That's what I did. In October I came back to Anchorage with over one thousand dollars, told Mom I was going to pay everything off and she could have the business.

Mom said, "Don, it's all paid off and I have money in the bank!" I couldn't believe it! I said, "MOM it's all yours!" I was a free man again. Mom had a few profitable years before they gave up the lease.

Anchorage Fur Rendezvous

There are a lot of different versions of how the Anchorage Fur Rendezvous got its start. The following is the truest account you will likely ever read.

At a basketball practice in about 1937, Clyde Conover, Vern Johnson and Dale Bowen decided to organize a basketball and hockey tournament. As officers of the Anchorage Athletic Association they were in control of the recently acquired funds that constituted the treasury of this organization. The merchants of Fairbanks had provided these funds in the following manner. The Anchorage city basketball and hockey teams were invited to play the Fairbanks city teams during the Fairbanks Winter Ice Carnival celebration. To help defray the travel costs they sent several books of raffle tickets, which were to be sold to the citizens of Anchorage, with the proceeds to be applied to travel expenses. Unfortunately, or fortunately, as you will see, these tickets were not saleable in the local market. Time to depart arrived and we still had the tickets. We paid our own way to Fairbanks and, of course, took the tickets along.

During a conference we filled out the stubs of the tickets with the Anchorage Athletic Association name and address. We then carefully folded the tickets several times, then straightened them out. This, we hoped, would make them easier to pick up out of the basket.

The result! We won a new Buick, a refrigerator, a console radio and numerous other prizes. In spite of our instant unpopularity with almost everyone, in Fairbanks, we were able to sell these items and return to Anchorage with our winnings. New basketball and hockey uniforms were ordered and the aforementioned trio organized an invitational basketball and hockey tournament for March. This was a success.

During the ensuing construction season, most of the basketball and hockey players left town to work. That fall, on their return to Anchorage, they learned that the Anchorage Athletic Association now included a baseball team. This baseball team, with new uniforms, had enjoyed a charter flight to Dawson City, Canada wiping out our treasury.

Another tournament was held the following spring, again a success. Later a fur auction was added along with boxing matches, the Miners and Trappers Ball, dog races, etc. and a new name was chosen. The Anchorage Fur Rendezvous.

Bob Dunn

Bob was old. That is, his body was old, but his mind and attitude were a few decades younger than his years. This contrast would sharpen when he had a nip of Johnny Walker Scotch.

We were in a Road Commission camp, way over in the Kuskokwim valley, in the Interior of Alaska, building a road from the river to the village of Takotna. We lived in tents, seven men each, worked seven days a week and shared the land with the birds, beasts and a hundred zillion mosquitoes.

Bob was bull cook. His job was to cut wood for the tents and cookshack and keep the water buckets full. Every month or so, Art Shonbeck, a rich business man and mine owner from Anchorage, would fly through McGrath, our supply center, about twenty miles from camp. While in McGrath he would always buy a quart of Johnny Walker. It would arrive at camp with the weekly mail boat. This was for his old friend, Bob.

Now Bob was always a pleasure to be around. He was the cleanest man in camp. His long underwear, which he wore summer and winter, would show at his open shirt and would be unbelievably white. His other clothes showed him to be King of Klean. Bob had short, curly white hair, a ruddy complexion in a nice round face, a big smile and the most alive, devilish eyes I have ever seen. Bob could make a Budda grin.

After one of the Shonbeck fly-bys we could expect that Bob would pop into our tent and give us a treat. Not the bottle, no one ever saw that. We only knew what Fred, the mechanic and supply boat driver, told us, "Yep, Bob's got another one. Watch out."

The first time I saw Bob in action was when he put on a scene from Shakespeare's "The Taming of the Shrew."

My tent had mostly young guys. We were lying on our cots, after dinner, when Bob pops through the tent flap and the show began. Bob set the stage by explaining that it was a scene with two actors, father and daughter. Greta Garbo, he explained, played the daughter. "She's a terrible actress. Here, I'll show you!"

We watched as this eighty-year-old sourdough, in his after dinner corduroy pants tucked into his unlaced shoepacs, suspenders over his lily white long johns, as he gave a flawless, several minute performance. Missing not a word, switching from basso Father to falsetto daughter as the lines changed. He squatted like he was sitting on the father's knee when he took the daughter's part. The father's voice resonant, projecting, perfect, "On this 'pointed day you and Petrucio should be married and yet, we see not of our son-in-law. What will be said—?

"No shame but mine, I must forthwith be forever—" the daughters voice was screeching, harshly abrasive, and the lines were delivered as though by a high school freshman. The magic was that he transported us, through his talent, to a great rendition of one of Shakespeare's finest works. I had never seen a professional stage play, but knew that I had seen, and heard, a magnificent performance. An unlikely audience, in an unbelievable setting was spellbound.

How could he put on such a brilliant performance? The word was that Bob had been on the stage in New York and had left to lose himself, in the Klondike gold rush in Alaska, after an altercation in which the other party had departed for the next world.

Other times, when his friend furnished fuel, Bob treated us to "Spartacus, " "Horatio at the Bridge" and other classics.

Bob lived in another tent. One of his tentmates was a "squaw man," named Anderson. Anderson suffered a constant barrage of harsh criticism because of his smelly feet. The odor would "gag a maggot," as the poet says. I heard Bob tell Anderson. "Here! Take this tablet and use it. I sent for it just so you could do something about those damn feet of yours. We can't stand it any more. Here, take it and use it!"

Anderson took the tablet and left.

A couple of days later I, again, heard Bob confront Anderson.

"Dammit! I told you to use that tablet. Your feet smell as rotten as ever. Why the hell didn't you use it?"

"I did! I took it right after you gave it to me."

"YOU WHAT?"

"I took it. Had a helluva time getting it down!"

"YOU SWALLOWED IT?"

"Yeah! Sure did!"

"You damn fool, you were supposed to put it into a tub of hot water and soak your feet."

We watched Anderson, for several days, expecting that he might die, but he didn't.

Bon Dunn's favorite saying was, "This world, the next, then the fireworks."

NEWS ITEM
Anchorage Times Newspaper, July 18, 1942

Bob Dunn, 85, Sourdough survivor of the Klondike Gold Rush, was struck by a car, and killed, while crossing 9th Ave.

Bob, now, is one step nearer the fireworks.

Charley

Charley was another sourdough hangover from the Klondike. Not a boozer, he just had been searching for 35 years for the big strike. Now he was around seventy and was a laborer in our Road Commission camp.

Charley didn't mingle. He had his own 7 by 9-foot tent and confined his contact with the rest of us to the cookshack and whomever he was working with. Charley was also our contact with the outside world. A six-volt car battery powered his radio. He had a little gasoline-powered generator to keep the battery charged. At breakfast and again at dinner, Charley would deliver a concise account of the happenings in Alaska, territory wide and the world. He gave us no opinions, did not orate, just informed us. Tall, rangy, slope shouldered, powerful, Charley could work with any of the younger men, whether falling trees, carrying corduroy logs or using a muckstick.

Charley's cabin was on the Kuskokwim River so he had a boat. He decided the boat was too short so brought it into camp, cut it in half. After Fred, our mechanic and supply boat driver, brought him some lumber, Charley added two feet to the middle of the boat. The whole operation was a little too much for me to believe.

In the evenings, Charley would turn on the radio, in his tent and listen to the news and programs like Amos and Andy. The very best, though, was on Saturday night when the Coconut Grove orchestra, with Phil Harris, came from Hollywood. Some of us younger guys would sit around on the stumps and rocks to listen to the sweet sounds and dream of finer things like baths, women, booze and good food.

We had shared several Saturday nights with the mosquitoes when, this time, a sudden, intense, rain shower hit us. Surprise! Surprise! Charley invited the four of us into his tent to hear the rest of the show. We crowded in and sat on the ground entrance, lost in our own melody fed fantasies, for over an hour. Phil Harris and his band were really great. They were so good that they moved Ed to say, "Gawd, that's beautiful!"

Charley erupted in rage, transformed with fury. "If you're going to talk, do it someplace else! OUT! OUT! All of YOU!"

We left hurriedly, and were never invited back.

Goal Driven

I met a guy who knew exactly, what he wanted to do with the rest of his life.

Grady was my swamper. His job was to do the handwork that arose while I operated the bulldozer, clearing the right of way. Grady was a farm boy from Texas with a tale to tell. He and his cousin had met Whitey in a bar at Amarillo. He told them he wanted to go to Nome, Alaska and mine gold. Whitey was short of funds, but full of stories about the wonders of Alaska and the gold on the beaches at Nome. Whitey did not tell them that the Nome gold rush had occurred some thirty-five years before.

The cousin's savings had brought the three of them to Anchorage, with just enough left for airfare to Nome. Trouble was, they had been weathered in at McGrath, halfway to Nome. Our Superintendent was in McGrath. We needed men in our crew. The trio desired to continue eating. They hired on.

Big enough to pull a stump by hand, good-natured but useless, Grady wound up as my swamper. In good going there would be very little for him to do so he would ride the drawbar of the tractor. He filled my ear with the wonders of Texas. His only talent, that I was aware of, was to imitate the squeal of the dozer winch. It sounded like the blade was slipping and dropping, so I would grab for the lever. He would then erupt with knee slapping laughter.

Grady's most important chore, as far as I was concerned, was to make my coffee for lunch. We had a one-gallon can with a bale on it. He would put the water in about eleven o'clock then attempt to have the coffee ready by twelve. So help me, he could not build a fire. I showed him how to break the small twigs at the bottom of the branches on the spruce trees, how to strip the bark off the birch trees, light it and carefully feed larger sticks until he had a good fire. Grady never mastered that skill so made a dozen trips to the dozer with his little can to get diesel oil to fan the flames. It was a funny-sad spectacle. Most of the time I got the coffee well after I had eaten my lunch.

On his better days he would ride the drawbar and sing western songs, but in cold, windy, wet weather, he would seek shelter under a spruce tree. He became a huge, huddled, homesick, little boy.

"OH! I was supposed to tell you about the guy who knew, exactly what he wanted to do with the rest of his life. It was Grady."

"Soon as I get enough money to get me back to Texas, I'm gone. I'm gonna plant my feet under my Pappy's table and I'll, damn sure, never, ever, leave again!"

Gus

Gus could lie on his cot for an hour or two, eyes open, fixed on something no one else could see, head immobile, his body almost tense. Sometimes he would break out with profanity in his Norwegian accented growl.

The stove in our tent was a fifty-gallon drum, lying flat on legs with a door in one end. Sometimes, when he was in his trance and one of us jerked the door open to add wood, Gus would fly off the bed ready for combat. He would stand there, confused, for a few seconds, grumble and lie back down.

Gus was one of the Sourdoughs, late sixties or maybe seventy, who had seen the Klondike Gold Rush, then had prospected all over the interior of Alaska for the thirty years since the big event.

These old guys in our crew would hole up in a cabin, living on rice, beans, bacon, moose and some of the game birds for the long Arctic winter. They were too old to trap very much, so welcomed a summer's work with the Road Commission. With luck they could make a stake of six or seven hundred dollars, for the five-month construction season. This would buy the staple food for the winter.

Gus was a laborer and spent most of that season shoveling the muck from the swamp up onto the corduroy logs. I then graded it down with the dozer so it could dry out. We graveled it and had a road (sort of).

Gus would come to work in the spring, lean and mean, with his Levis and shirts hanging on his big boned frame. At that time he was a big pain at the eating table. He wanted all the food and right now. If he could possibly reach it he would, sometimes almost climbing on the table. If he asked you to pass a platter, his hand would be out at arm's length, fingers opening and closing like gimme! gimme! NOW!

If Gus had room on his plate he would take all on the platter, not just some, all of it. One time he dumped a whole platter of canned sausages on his hotcakes. The dammed things were almost indigestible at best and then in small quantities. Gus spent a couple of days in bed and agony, but survived. By season's end Gus had filled out his generous frame, developed his huge belly and was ready for the coming winter.

Gus was strong. We were building a bridge across a stream. Even though he was seventy, he picked up one end of a fourteen-foot steel I-beam, walked across another one and set his end down. Another guy and I were handling the near end.

Gus and I were alone in the tent one evening. He asked me what it was like out in the States. He hadn't been south of Anchorage in over twenty years. I told him about some of it and answered his questions. It came out that he wanted to go to Portland and buy a movie theater. I had heard that Gus was an exception to most old prospectors and actually had about $50,000. That was a helluva lot of money at that time.

Gus said that was what he thought about all the time. Buying a theater in Portland. His worry was that he would be cheated and lose his nest egg. We talked for quite a while with me trying to convince him to buy an annuity so that his investment would be safe. He would get so much a month for the rest of his life.

Well, that was a good idea, he said. I could see though that the theater dream was what he really wanted to see come true. I was sure that shortly after he arrived in Portland he would be a plucked pigeon.

"You want to know how Gus ended up? So do I!" I never saw Gus again after that season.

Teamwork

Gene and Shorty detested each other. They had a real lip curling, grunt-growl relationship. Gene, on the tractor, pulled Shorty on a heavy old road grader, so some teamwork was required.

Gene was tall, well over six feet. In his mid-20s, he was a powerful 230-pound farm boy. Congenial, good company.

Shorty was a 70-year-old sourdough whose smirking, toothless face was deformed by a huge wad of Peerless tobacco in his left cheek. This was removed only briefly at meal times, when he would pick and fuss at his food. Never did spit. Slept on his right side so he got full benefit from the Kentucky leaf. Small but tough, he could bust your butt on the other end of a bucksaw, grinning all through the ego-shattering encounter.

We had been working seven days a week building road, in the Kuskokwim River Valley, in Alaska, with poor food, seven men to a tent, in mosquito-filled isolation. After five months, this can be wearing on the disposition. Something had triggered Gene and Shorty's contempt for each other. I was not in on the beginning of their trouble, but I saw the explosive end.

At breakfast that day the boss looked over at me. "How're you doin' on that fill?"

"I'll finish this morning," I said.

"Good, I'll start Gene and Shorty at the landing. They should be up to you by noon."

I nodded and looked over at Gene. The color was coming up through his neck and cheeks. Bad news. Gene and Shorty hadn't worked together for more than a week and were almost back to being human.

Shorty shoved his plate away, reached for his Peerless and stormed out of the cookshack. Finished eating, I came out to find Gene and Shorty facing each other.

Gene grunted, "Are you ready?"

Shorty scowled, "I'm always ready, plowboy!"

Gene checked a swing and headed for the rigs. I headed for my dozer.

Out at the site, I had finished the fill and was dressing up the slope when the happy pair arrived. They had started down the left side of the fill when not paying attention, Shorty screwed up and let the blade of the grader dig in too deep. This threw the rear wheels very close to the edge of the fill. Because this momentous event occurred long before hydraulic or electronic controls, Shorty had to spin the large control wheels to raise the blade. That's a slow process; Shorty had no time... The grader was slipping closer and closer to the edge. Much more and it would flip.

Now is the time for you to guess how this wondrous dilemma could be resolved. Yes, Gene had to look back, see the problem and stop the tractor. Most tractor-grader combos were in constant visual contact. But Gene never looked back at the miserable, mouthy little SOB. Hadn't for weeks. I watched as Shorty finally gave up on the wheel, jumped to the ground, grabbed the end of the blade in an attempt to hold a 6500 pound hunk of machinery from rolling over.

Shorty's 130 pounds, of course, had no effect whatever, so when the grader flipped, Shorty rocketed skyward 15 or more feet. Arms and legs flailing wildly, he had a brief but spectacular flight.

When the grader flipped, the Cat lurched. Gene looked back, shut her down, and then stepped to the ground. Shorty flew at him like a wildcat. Gene met him with a straight right arm to the chest, grabbing a fistful of Hickory shirt. Shorty cussed and swung but couldn't connect. He landed a couple of kicks, so Gene spun him, grabbed the back of his collar with the left hand, his belt with the right. Now he held Shorty at arm length.

Tobacco juice is not adequate fuel for long combat. Shorty wound down. Gene released his grip, and Shorty, his strut a little jerky, headed for camp.

He never looked back. It was gin-clear to all: the working partnership was over.

Paavo

Paavo had been part of the crew for several weeks before I got aquatinted with him. Small guy maybe 5' 7" and 150 pounds, but from watching him with an ax, all man. He never buddied with any of the guys, was always pleasant and friendly, but had one major problem, he could barely speak English. The word was that he was a Finlander.

We were in the Kuskokwim Valley, in the heart of Alaska, building a fifteen-mile road from the river to Takotna. Several of the crew were Klondikers so in 1937 were in their seventies and working for beans and rice for the winter. Paavo was younger, maybe late fifties.

One day the boss said, "Grady said he's too sick to work today. Paavo will be your swamper."

I was a bulldozer operator. After the fallers and slashers had knocked the trees down I would bulldoze stumps, trees and brush off the right of way. The going was good. I could drop the blade at the centerline, cut through the moss to the permafrost and move a helluva bunch of trees, roots and brush, leaving behind a hard frozen earth that would eventually be a road.

As swamper it was Paavo's job to move sticks, roots etc. that I had missed, out to the pile. Another duty was to make coffee for our lunch. He was a quick study and did his part with no direction. At noon he had a fire going and the coffee on when I shut down the rig.

While we ate we tried to talk, but I had a helluva time understanding him. Finally he rolled off a couple of sentences that made me aware that it was in French. Francais, I think he said. I couldn't help him there that's for sure. I did get to know that he was not a trapper or a prospector.

A week or so later Grady had enough money to get back to Texas and put his feet under his pappy's table, "Never, ever to leave again!" So I wound up with Paavo once more. I liked the guy. He had a pleasant personality, eyes alive with life and a great smile flashing perfect teeth. We got better at understanding each other after a few days. I learned that he was nearly sixty, had been in America five years, four in Alaska.

"What do you do in the winter time?" I asked.

"Same, chop wood."

"All winter?"

"Yes, all winter."

" What do you do with the wood?"

"Riverboat!" he rotates his hands like a paddle wheel.

The paddlewheel riverboats were still running then. They were steam driven so required enormous amounts of wood for their boilers. There were stations at appropriate locations where the steamers could stop and take on more fuel. Traveling the river you would see great stacks of four-foot long logs piled to a height of four feet. That made it easy to determine the quantity, as every eight feet of length would be a cord. These piles could run for hundreds of yards along the bank.

"That's what you do? Cut wood for the riverboats?"

"Yes, Yes. All winter."

"By yourself? Just you? Alone?"

"Yes, me!"

I'm thinking, my God what a way to make a living.

"How long? How many years?"

He holds up four fingers says "Years!"

"How do you get the logs out of the woods?"

I didn't reach him with that one, so I went through the motions of chopping down a tree, limbing it and then acting like I was carrying it to the river. "Maybe you have dogs?"

"No dogs! Dogs eat ver' much!" He acted like he was tying a rope to the log, then went through the motion of throwing the rope over his shoulder and pulling the log.

"You mean you neck the logs out of the woods to the pile?" He nods.

"Wouldn't you rather do something else? Change jobs?"

"No change jobs! Good job, ver' happy!'

Shaking my head I said, "Why in hell would you stay with that? Why?"

"Round world!" He makes a circle with his hand.

Puzzled I say, "Yeah, the world is round."

"Me, Paavo, round world! First Class!"

This stops me. "You go around the world?"

"Yes! Yes! First Class! Work jobs two years. Me, Paavo, go round world. Big, big ship! First Class!" He stands up and brings both hands to shoulder height drops them to indicate fine clothing. Goes through the motions of ordering the wine and approving it with all the flourishes. Suddenly, I have a vision. I can see Paavo; immaculate in evening dress, in the dining salon with two gloriously gowned lovelies. Seating them, assisting them with the menu, consulting with the Wine steward and then tasting the chosen vintage and nodding assent.

"How many times? " I ask.

"Two."

Sixty years later I'm still stunned by Paavo's world.

Turnip Mike

Mike hiked the Klondike, along with a few thousand other gold hungry guys in the year 1897.

Forty years later in 1937, when I met him, his search came to an end. In the intervening years he had prospected and survived. Nothing more. Now, in his seventies, he was sitting on some claims, hundreds of miles from the big discovery on Bonanza Creek, which had proven value. They had been worked by a dredge, years before, then been abandoned.

The Strandberg brothers were working the claims on Candle Creek just up stream from Mike. They were using a new fangled method, namely a dragline. They ignored the tailings, left from the dredge operation, just removing them as overburden. They then dug up the bedrock, which they processed through an elevated sluice box. It was a very profitable operation. Mike had an agreement with the Strandberg's that they would work his claims on a percentage basis.

The present season would see the end of the work on the Strandberg claims so they would start on Mikes after the following Spring thaw. In the meantime Mike was a bull cook at the Strandberg camp. He cut wood, kept the water pails full at the cook shack and did whatever had to be done.

The old, gold rushers always fascinated me. There were still a lot of them around in 1937. Most were in their seventies. The ones I met, of course, were the unsuccessful ones. Never had made the big find. Some had made and lost small fortunes. They would work enough for a stake, then head for the creeks.

Mike invited me into his cabin one evening. The centerpiece

of the room was a table about four feet square which was covered, except for a space for a plate, cup, saucer and a frying pan, with dozens and dozens of small medicine bottles. He had a complete drug store right there at his fingertips. Enough to keep him going.

Now, I really took a good look at Mike. Of course he wore shoepacs, with scuffed rubber bottoms and unlaced leather uppers, just the laces tied around his ankles. Had for forty years, except in the really cold weather. Worn, red suspenders held up tin pants, stained and stiff enough to stand alone. A clean, black and red plaid shirt tucked in at the waist. Under the shirt, at the throat, shined out clean, white long johns. A pale, frail neck wrinkled its way up to a lean, bony, white stubble covered chin. A wide mouth with double dentures, hung under an oversize Roman nose. Mikes eyes, fading blue, were wary, spelled maybe, weary. Bristly brows underlined a deeply furrowed forehead, which supported the iron gray, tousled mop of hair. Mike's ears, both big, had heard it all for seventy some years. Large hands no longer able to control the pick, shovel, and ax expertly, were now capable only of aiding survival.

We talked for a while of the old days. Bonanza Creek and Dawson City, Chicken, the Nome beaches, Cripple Creek. He had been to them all.

"Mike, you been alone all these years? Ever been married?"

"Yeah, sorta!"

"How can you be sorta married?"

"Happened in Dawson during the Rush. We were in Maybelle's joint. There was this young lady that was thinking about turning out—going to work there. I told her she could put her shoes under my bed anytime. We were all pretty drunk, 'cept her, and especially me, I guess. I came to back on the creek and they told me I was married to that young lady. My buddies had helped her get us married, then lugged me back to the boat and the creek."

"How'd it turn out?"

"Never saw her again. She sent word she needed some money so I sent her a couple hundred. Later on her mother got sick back in Indiana, so I sent her all I had so she could go home. But that's all yesterdays. It's been a long time a-comin'. I've eaten a lot of beans, rice, bacon and sourdough, but now it's the gravy train. One more season after this and I'm on my way outside for good."

Mike didn't make it to the spring thaw.

"Why did they call him Turnip Mike?"

"Well, wherever Mike built a cabin, and settled for a year or so, he always planted a garden. He had left abandoned garden patches all over the interior of Alaska. The turnips came up whether Mike was there or not."

The Wages of Sin

George's past, before the last couple of years, was a mystery to the crew. We had heard that he had raised a family, in Colorado, beyond that nothing.

Since coming to Alaska he had worked, for a couple of seasons, in the mining camps and now was a laborer on our crew. George was a nice looking man, kept himself clean. He shaved regularly. A ladies man? Yeah, well sort of. It was his practice, at season's end, to take his stake and move into an agreeable whorehouse, not to surface 'til he was sober, broke and had worn out his welcome, among other things.

A quirk in his personality caused him to be the dirtiest talking man I had ever been around. Working with road building crews you get used to obscenity, but nothing like George's. I told him one time that his mind was a cesspool that accumulated all the filth around and that it gushed from his mouth in an incredibly detestable tirade. He made no response to the insult.

As a laborer he was expected to set choker to pull the stumps, cut and carry twenty-foot pieces of corduroy logs for the road. The logs were, usually, six to eight inches in diameter, of green spruce or birch and a real struggle, for one man on each end to carry them out of the woods over the swamp and lay them side by side on the roadway. It would take at least a hundred and fifty to make a one hundred feet of road. Then each side had to be ditched and the swamp gunk shoveled on the logs to dry. Leveled and graveled you had a pioneer road of sorts.

George lasted two months before his legs gave out and he could not work. The boss had to lay him off. He hung around camp for a couple of days until the next mail run with the supply boat would take him to McGrath.

At 19, I felt sorry for the old reprobate, but figured he was reaping the rewards of a misspent life. I was not going to wind up like George that's for sure. My Dad had lost everything in the "Crash of '29", he took us out of a mining town so us four boys wouldn't die of miners consumption. We struggled to eat and now I was making good money. Some would be there when I was old George's age. Damn Right! When it came time for George to leave we all chipped in and gave him enough money to get to Fairbanks and eat for a couple of weeks 'til he got his check from the Road Commission.

It was four or five months before the season ended and I was back in Anchorage. We hung around the Club Bar a lot. There would be no work 'til spring so we shot pool, drank and partied most of the winter with guys we had worked with here and there. I had thought a lot about George and was curious to learn if he was dead or what had happened to him. I did learn that George had gone to Fairbanks, then written to a waitress friend in Seattle. She had sent him money to come to the States and he moved in with her.

"My God, I thought, what a dismal way to go!" It was one he had chosen though. Several months later I was recalling old times in the Kuskokwim with a buddy and the subject of George came up. We discussed the probable scenario of him winding up sleeping in the streets of Seattle, on Skid Row. We got more sentimental with each beer. By midnight we were certain that George would probably die in some alley in Seattle.

"Hi guys!" It was Shorty. He had worked with us and, of course, George on the Takotna Road. "What's up?"

"We were just feeling sorry for George, figure he must be down and out or dead by now."

"Oh no! Hadn't you heard? Some relative of George's he never knew, died and left him two and a half million dollars. He and his gal are living it up. Bought a penthouse, doing cruises, the whole works, Lucky Bastard!"

We Met

We met on the SS Baranof, Seattle to Seward, May 1940. I was heading back to Anchorage after a luxurious winter in Santa Barbara. She was on her way to Cordova, for a seasonal job. First time I saw this lovely brunette in the lounge I was smitten. When the band started I strolled over. "May I have this dance?" Consulting her program, she said, "You may have the eighth. What is your name?"

"Don. What's yours?"

"Just call me Bobbie."

In them days, women in Alaska were scarce and just getting a dance was a good start. The next three days we played Ping-Pong on a rolling ship, danced, and I even showed her the engine room. (The Rotterdam it was not.) Bobbie got off the ship at Cordova.

In Anchorage my mother met me with, "Road Commission called. You are to take a Star Airlines plane out at seven in the morning, to Candle Landing." I was broke so I went.

I crawled into the big, old single engine Pilgrim. Chet, the pilot, said, "No seats. Make a place in the cargo." We flew through Rainy Pass, across the Alaska Range to the Kuskokwim Valley and landed at McGrath. A waiting Bellanca set me down on a high hilltop near the road. Sitting on a stump, I watched the Bellanca disappear in the snowstorm.

"Don! Don! What in the hell are you doing here?" Ten days ago it was Santa Barbara, nice apartment, sun, sand, surf, yellow Packard roadster, friendly females and then Barbara and the boat. Now I faced seven months, seven days a week, seven men to a tent, one lousy battery-radio in the whole camp, mosquitoes by the zillions, camp-cook food, pushing trees and dirt with a dozer. Bleak future.

After a week or so I wrote to Bobbie. "If you'll come to Anchorage after the season ends, I'll quit my job and go to Anchorage where they were building Fort Richardson. I think that would be great!" I didn't get an answer. Shipboard romance and so forth and so forth—six weeks later there is a letter. Her answer had come to Anchorage, was sent back to Seattle where it caught a once a month Coast Guard Cutter to Bethel. There it was transferred to a paddle-wheel riverboat. It traveled several hundred miles up the Kuskokwim River to McGrath. Our weekly supply boat brought it to camp.

Looking at the letter, I said to myself, "Well, Don old boy, you did make an impression!" Big deal. "Dear sir, I think I do remember you. You are the blond who doesn't dance too well. I have decided to come to Anchorage because the job market is better there. I will see you, maybe."

It came to pass that we went together for several months. We decided to get married. She decided before I did.

We were in her little apartment one night. "Now that we're getting married, we will need a few things..." Picking us a Sears catalogue, she went from one earmarked page to another, punctuating the action with, "We'll need some of these—aren't these darling—Oh! Yes, we will have to have, at least four..."

I was still trying to calm my stomach after hearing the word "Married."

"And six of these!" she said.

"Why don't you just put your name and address on the cover, send it in and say you'll take the whole package?"

Suddenly supersonic, the Sears sailed by my head and smashed the wall.

"I knew, right then, our marriage would never last.

(Did though. We're on our fifty-eighth year.)

Salesman

"Well, I guess, if you want to sell the damn piano, you have to keep punching doorbells 'til somebody wants to buy it or you can talk them into buying it!" I was talking to myself. We were on the outskirts of Shelton. I had been ringing doorbells for six or seven hours, when we hit pay dirt—maybe!

"How did I get into this situation?"

I had been in Alaska for five years building roads, in season, six months or so in the brush with just the cook and crew. Now I was newly married, wanted to enjoy the warm, snuggly life of love and kisses. This meant a new occupation. I needed to learn how to talk to people without every third word being an obscenity.

We had been walking down the street in Port Angeles. The sign in the window said, "Piano Salesman Wanted." Opportunity knocks for Don!

J. B. was a partner in the business. Small, ex-Olympic diver, but now sixty or so. Not crooked, but cute in the manipulation sometimes required to make a sale. I liked him so agreed to try selling, commission basis, and I had the whole Olympic Peninsula as my territory.

They furnished a small, enclosed trailer and the pianos. I provided the car, gas, paid all my own expenses like food, hotels, etc. On reflection I don't think it was such a good deal, we starved a lot, but I was sure learning to talk nice.

Back to Shelton and the gentle lady who answered the door.

"Yes, Yes. She had wanted a piano all her married life. Hadn't been possible 'cause George was a construction superintendent, yah know! He was now retired so maybe he would buy her one!"

I went in, and she drug George from somewhere, and I went into my spiel. The piano was repossessed (it wasn't), was in perfect shape (it was), I could sell it at a great price, on reasonable terms. George and I jawed back and forth for a half-hour, or so, with the Mrs. interjecting, "George you promised me, George!" every few moments. Finally George said, "O.K., Margie, if you will promise me that you can play as well as this guy, after one year, I'll buy the damn thing!"

"Oh! I will, I will!" she exclaimed.

I wasted no time. Hurried out to the car, loaded the Piano on the dolly and Bobbie and I brought it in. There was no place to put it! George and Margie were storing all their daughter's furniture, while they were building a new home.

Finally we re-arranged the furniture, stacking some to the ceiling, and found wall space for the Spinet. Once that was done I filled out the contract. He signed and the deal was sealed. Almost!

"O.K.! Let's hear you play!"

Pucker time! I had never learned to play the piano. Oh! When I was eight or nine my mom signed me up for lessons. The teacher always sent me home 'cause my hands were too dirty or I wouldn't practice my lesson. Didn't learn much. J.B. had taught me to play the first two bars of Massenet's Elegy. I would play that, remark about the beautiful tone of the Baldwin, then go into the closing.

"C'mon, let's hear you play!"

I gave him Massenet and turned to talk.

"Play, don't talk!"

"That's all I know!"

"What the hell do you mean, That's all you know?"

"Sir, that is really all I can play!"

"God Dammit! Take that thing and get out of here!"

"Now George, you promised! I'll practice and practice, really I will!"

George shrugged, went into the kitchen. We heard the water running. Heard the glass fill and then the calump as he set it down. We waited several more minutes. George returned.

Looking at Margie he said, "OK, Honey."

I stood—he reluctantly shook hands. I left.

J.B. had told me, "Every buyer suffers 'buyers remorse' even if it is trading their money for something like a comb. The bigger the bite the more they feel it. Never go back, for the follow up call, for two weeks. By then they will be happy with their purchase." Margie waited three weeks.

Iturbi

Mary and Dave were a rare couple. What I call instant old time friends.

Bobbie and I were in Manette (now east Bremerton). I had canvassed the area and Mary had answered the door at 1110 Ironside Ave. I gave her the spiel about the repossessed piano. She and Dave had just retired and had discussed getting a piano for Mary. She had been active in music while in school, but had neglected that area of her life while raising children. They were on their own wings now so she was ready to buy.

Bobbie and I brought the spinet into the home. They were happy with the price and terms so—!

"Don, I have to call my brother. He is a concert pianist and would never forgive me for buying without consulting him. Let me call him and have him come over!"

"Fine, Mary, I want you to be completely happy about your purchase."

We visited with Dave while Mary was making the call. Mary returns. "Sidney is busy giving a lesson, but will come over when he is free. Probably an hour or so, will that be alright?"

"Oh sure, that's fine."

Mary brought out some snacks and lemonade so we chatted the time away.

Sidney arrived with a flourish. He was immaculate in a Tux. No time for introductions to us. "What kind of piano did you say it was?"

"It's a Baldwin, Sidney. There it is."

"Oh, yes I see. Tiny little thing isn't it?"

I'm thinking, "Damn! - Damn! - What have we here?"

Sidney sits down at the piano, strikes a few chords and says, "It's out of tune, not bad, but out!" He launches into a few exercises while I am explaining to Mary, and I hope to Sidney, that our piano tuner will be making a trip through this area within a couple of weeks. He will then stop by and fine-tune the instrument.

Sidney, a masterful artist, gave us a recital that others would be paying a large sum, later that evening, to enjoy. He must have played for twenty minutes, really giving that little Acrosonic a time to remember. We sat entranced then—"Well Mary, it's not top quality. Not really a Steinway, that's for sure. I couldn't really recommend your buying it. How much is it?"

Mary told him.

"Mary a piano is a lifetime investment. You should get a good piano if you are going to invest that much money. None of the leading artists use a Baldwin. They all use Steinway."

"Geez!" I'm thinking. "This guy is wiping me out. She will not go against him."

I dig in my briefcase and find the book with the testimonials in it. Haven't more than glanced at it myself.

"Sir" I say, "These concert pianists all use the Baldwin!"

"Who are they?"

I start reading off the names of the various artists that play the Baldwin Concert Grand Piano. Sidney makes a comment after each name. "No talent! Nothing there. Should play in a carnival. "

"Jose Iturbi!" I call out.

"Jose Iturbi! I don't believe it!"

"Yes, I say. It's right here!"

Sidney grabs the book. Utter silence while Sidney absorbs the glowing testimonials by Mr. Iturbi. Sidney, deflated and almost human is silent for several minutes. We await the verdict from on high.

"Sidney, I won't be playing recitals. I leave that up to you. I just want a nice piano I can enjoy."

"Well Mary, I guess it would be okay. If that's what you want."

Bobbie and I sat there waiting for the full drama to unfold. Will we continue eating or will Sidney put us on another diet.

"It's not a Steinway, but it may be all you need. I have a concert so must leave. Bye Dave. Tah tah Mary. See you later!"

The jerk didn't even acknowledge Bobbie and I.

We signed the papers and welcomed two new friends to our relationships. We would later see more of Mary and Dave.

All that Glitters

I was in the store one day when a couple walked in. Lois, J.B.'s wife, was busy so I asked if I could help them.

"We want a piano, but we haven't much money, so we're shopping."

"We have one that you may be interested in!" (I'm thinking, "I doubt it!")

J.B. had taken in a "Clunker." That meant it was an old upright, instead of the new spinet. This one was in really bad shape as far as appearance went. He tuned it and it was OK. He then filled the gouges with wood putty, sanded it some and then painted it with aluminum paint. I saw him putting on the finishing touches. He was tossing glitter into the wet paint.

"We'll sell it to some honky tonk!" he said.

I led the couple back through the new spinets. Waving at the glamorous, glittering masterpiece, I said, "You might be interested in this!"

"OH! I love it!" The lady exclaimed. "Don't you just love it, John!"

He got a kinda silly grin on his face. "It would be different! Is it in good shape?"

I ran a finger over the keys. "Just tuned, sounds good doesn't it?"

"Do you play?" I asked.

"I do!" the lady said.

I got the bench and she sat down. Played "Red Sails in the Sunset" and a couple of other tunes. "Sounds good to me," she said.

"How much is it?" John asked.

"One hundred thirty-five." I said. (Remember, this was 1941.)

"Oh John! Let's take it!"

"OK. but we will have to have it delivered."

"Where to?"

"Sapho."

"That will be an extra fifteen dollars."

"All right."

I took them up front, explained the agreement to Lois. She wrote up the papers and we agreed on the delivery time. Because I had made the sale I would get a commission of ten dollars. I would make the delivery so would get the fifteen dollars. Twenty-five bucks! Not Bad!

On delivery day we loaded the clunker in the trailer. Bobbie and I set out for Sapho. We found their house, it was a small two-room cabin. Bobbie and I put the piano on the dolly. John wasn't there so I muscled it up on their wooden walkway, with Bobbie handling the dolly. It took us a while to get it into the house, but at last we made it.

The lady pointed where she wanted it so I took it there, tilted it up so Bobbie could take the dolly. When I did this the back caster gave way so, with the dolly gone, it sat at a tilt.

"Bobbie, put the dolly back." I hoisted the piano again. Swinging it around I could see that the block, with the caster on it, had slid up between the two posts it had been glued to.

"No problem!" I said. What an understatement!

"Do you have a hand drill?"

The lady was almost in shock. "No, I'm afraid we haven't!"

"Okay, I'll see if I can get one."

After knocking on several doors I was able to borrow a hand drill, a screwdriver, and a three-inch wood screw. Back at the problem, I could see that the gal was distraught. Bobbie was reassuring her.

"He'll fix it!" Bobbie said.

"Do you have a hammer?"

She fluttered one from the kitchen. I pounded the block back down, took the hand drill, then angled a hole through the block into the post. Soaping the screw and driving it in made a repair that all hell couldn't loosen.

I rolled the piano back in place, jacked it up. Bobbie took the dolly. We said "Thank you very much" and departed.

J.B. told me the piano had probably been in a flood and the glue had given way.

Upstairs?

Bobbie and I were in Paulsbo. We had been several days without a sale. I had started punching doorbells at 9 A.M. Now at 3:30 I was looking at a house a good hundred and fifty feet back from the gate. If I could sell the damn piano, how would I get it into the house over the gravel walkway?

"Here goes!" I said to Bobbie.

"Luck!" she replied.

The door opened to a stocky red headed lady, probably just under sixty. She said, "Yes?"

"Ma'am, I am a representative of the Baldwin Piano Company. I have just repossessed an Acrosonic Spinet piano. You know one of the new, smaller pianos. It is in perfect condition and it can be had for a very reasonable price."

"A piano! You have a piano! Mercy me!"

"Yes Ma'am. It's in the trailer there."

"Hmm! I've been thinking of a piano for Mary Jo. Her mother, my sister, God rest her soul, just passed away and the girl is living with me."

Mrs. Malloy agreed to come out to the trailer to see the piano. I went back out, opened the flap, unstrapped the piano, set aside the blanket and was sitting on the bench when she came out. A brief demonstration and we had an agreement. I filled out the contract, she signed it, then said, "I will give you a check when you bring it into the house."

"Is your husband around?"

"I am a widow lady some five years now!"

"Would you have any scrap lumber?

She gave me a puzzled stare then said, "There may be some in the back, in the shed."

I retrieved four pieces of shiplap about six feet long. Bobbie would lay two of them down on the walkway, we would roll the piano a ways then she would lay the other two pieces. Struggling mightily we shuttled the shiplap and the piano up to the porch, and in the door.

I called, "Mrs. Malloy, where would you like me to put the Piano?"

She answered from another room. "Upstairs!"

"Upstairs? Oh! We can't do that!"

She appeared, hands on hips, chin thrust forward. "Take it back then! I can't put it up there myself!"

"Geez!" Bobbie and I needed that sale. We had a strong desire to keep on eating.

The stairway was fairly wide. Maybe 40 inches, the treads 10 inches or so. I counted the risers. Thirteen! Was that an omen? Bobbie was an expert at moving and placing the dolly. We decided to try it. We wheeled the piano over to the stairway. I put the leading edge on the highest step it would reach. I then lifted the piano high so that Bobbie could put the two front wheels on the next step. I would then push the piano forward till the leading edge reached the step above. This tricky, exhausting maneuver was repeated over and over, with me holding most of the weight of the Piano, constantly fighting the image of me at the bottom of the steps with one Baldwin Acrosonic piano resting on my mangled body. Finally, God rewarded us with the summit of our Everest.

"Put it in the large room at the end of the hall. That's Mary Jo's room. Put it between the windows."

"Ma'am, a piano should always be placed on an inside wall, then it won't draw moisture!"

"All right, Dearie, put it over here then."

That done, she said, "Thank you dear boy, and you too

young lady!"

I'm standing there holding the dolly. She looked at me, puzzled.

"The check Ma'am."

"Oh! Of course." She reached in her apron pocket and brought forth our means to eat for another week.

"Thank you very much. Don't forget to return the boards to the back yard."

"Uh! Yes, Ma'am."

The Last Chord

We were in Aberdeen. J.B. was working one side of the street while I punched the doorbells on the other. A young lady, probably twenty-five, said she might be interested in a new piano. She invited me in and went over to her piano. It was an old Kimball upright. Striking some keys she said, "See, it's out of tune. It will not hold a tuning anymore!"

I nodded. I couldn't really tell whether it was off or not, but I said, "Yes, it really is irritating when it's off key. I'm sure you would be happy with the little Baldwin Acrosonic I have just repossessed. It's in beautiful condition. Just like new."

Just then her mother came into the room. "Now Sylvia, you just don't need a new piano. You should get it tuned. It will be fine!"

"Mother! It just won't hold a tune anymore. It's big and ugly too!"

"But dear, it's been in the family for years and years!"

"That's the problem, MOTHER!"

I was busy checking the piano. Keys OK. I raised the top and checked the strings and pads, pulled it away from the wall and checked the sounding board.

"We could give you a fair price for this as a trade in on the new one. I can bring it in and you will be able to see what a beautiful instrument it is. You know, many of the great concert artists use the Baldwin because of the pure rich tone it offers.

"Yes, I'd like to see it!"

"Sylvia! Think about it!"

"Hush, Mom!"

I went to the door, spotted J.B and waved. He saw me and came over. I threw the tarp, which was the back door of the trailer, up on the roof, unstrapped the piano and we put it on a dolly and wheeled it up into the living room.

"Oh! It's beautiful, and so much smaller!" She sat down and started to play.

"Isn't that a great full tone and so true in pitch!" I said. She nodded and kept playing.

J.B. was checking the clunker. "Seventy-five" he decided.

When Sylvia stopped, I said, "We can give you seventy-five dollars on the trade in. That leaves a balance of $325.00. Your monthly payment wouldn't be so much. You would have this lovely piano to enjoy!"

"Sylvia, think of it! That is a lot of money. The piano has been in the family for years. You don't need a new one!"

"Mother you gave it to me! I want a better one!"

"Well, I don't think you should!"

Sylvia looked at me. "I'll take it!"

"Fine," I said. I filled out the contract and she signed it. All this time J.B. was trying to mollify the mother.

We put the old piano on the dolly, moved the spinet into its place, then went out the door, down the steps, down the walk, off the curb and stopped behind the trailer. All this time the mother was yammering at us. "You shouldn't do this! Take it back. Sylvia doesn't know what she's doing. You should not take advantage of her! —On and on...

I was standing behind the piano, waiting while J.B. was trying to throw the tarp up on top. Being only five foot six, or so, he was having a hard time so I released the piano and went to help him.

Mother's jaw was still going a mile a minute, "That's a fine old piano. Bring it back, we must keep it!"

As I swung the tarp the most incredibly loud chord you can imagine assailed our ears. Because the road was crowned the piano was at an angle, so that when I released it gravity took over. The piano was lying on its face in the street.

Mother gasped, then wide-eyed spun and headed for the house. Sale completed.

Cavity

Everything one does has a consequence. As I was telling my granddaughter, "Even if you fart."

Well, this is about a fault my buddy Eddie Boyce had. He failed to brush his teeth properly so wound up with a cavity. That cavity launched me on a path that eventually had me sitting at the controls of a CC4A glider, crossing the German lines, over the Rhine River in World War II. We would land six miles back of the front in very hostile country. Improbable as this might seem to you that it is the absolute truth.

My career as an airman in the great conflict was full of stops, starts, twists and turns. To begin with I was supposed to be a fighter pilot. That's what I aimed for. If someone was going to be shooting at me I wanted it to be out in the open where I could see what this dude had working for him. Between him and me. No bullet in the back from a perch in a tree. My mind was back in World War I with Baron Von Ricthoven and the boys.

I had just passed my first physical to join the Cadets of the Army Air Corps when the Captain said, "Let me take another look at that eye."

I knew enough to say, "Yes Sir!"

"Hmm, that pterigium on your cornea will have to come off. It will eventually affect your vision. Have it removed, come back and you will be fine."

This was my first obstacle in my attempt to be noble and serve my country. My wife, Bobbie, and I scrounged up enough money for an operation. When I went back for my examination there was a new Captain.

"You've had an operation on your eye. Sorry, we can't use you."
"But--but!" My first lesson about the Army.

Later I was offered the chance to join the Civilian Pilot Training program. Still patriotic, etc., so I joined up and was paid $25.00 a month. I kept five and sent the rest to my pregnant Bobbie.

I went through Primary, Secondary, and Cross-country courses. The program was then changed to the War Training Service and our pay was upped to $50.00 per month. This was where I met Mr. Eddie Boyce. We were within one week of completing Instructor Finisher Course when half of the whole, goddam program shut down. We were all transferred to Kearns Field, near Salt Lake City, Utah to await further orders.

Because they had no productive training to offer we were handed over to the drill sergeants. We marched, marched, then we marched again, endlessly.

My feet, deficient of all the proper attributes of a normal healthy foot (flat arches, double-jointed toes, etc.), developed calluses under the metatarsal arch that made walking extremely painful. It was like having a rock in your shoe under the ball of your foot. Marching destroyed any resiliency that had ever been in the feet. I had decided that I would not march another damn step. "Bring on the Bastille, I say no more Marching!" Enter providence and Eddie's cavity.

The bulletin board listed the final group of students that would continue flight training. They would ship out to Yakima, Washington for Instrument Flight Training. Eddie Boyce was the last name listed to ship out.

    Eddie Boyce
    Don Conover
    Sam Small
    Hector Sousa
    Etc.

There was a mandatory physical required before the candidates could ship out.

I was sitting on my bunk when Eddie came in. "You won't believe this. They won't let me go 'til I get a goddam cavity filled. That means I'll never go. This is the last group that will continue flight training!"

Don moves up, passed the physical, eventually becomes a Glider Pilot Hero!

I wonder what ever happened to Eddie. We were told that the next duty, for those left behind, would be the infantry, so Eddie could have walked the war. Maybe wound up as a General.

Spot Landings

We were in transition training, from power aircraft to gliders, at night with only a string of oil flare pots to show the landing area and the spot. I don't, really, know how many successful landings had to be accomplished but I do remember a couple which were not successful.

Picture this—You are in a PT19 (low wing, two place, open cockpit airplane) at 500 feet, in a black Texas sky. You look down to your left and there is a line of the oil wick flare pots flickering away. The object is to spot land between number one and number two flares. You cut the throttle opposite the spot, establish the glide, and continue on the downwind leg. Judgment tells you when to start the base, then turn on final. You come in over the fence (literally, a barbed wire one). You continue to settle, the spot goes by, you continue to glide then thump, you touch down.

The problem? The ground falls away at the same rate as your glide angle. Next time come in lower but REMEMBER THE FENCE!

One guy comes in high, pancakes the airplane over the spot at twenty feet, and breaks the airplane in two. Washout.

You come in again and AAH! Hit the spot. Again you're lucky and your assignment is completed.

The next morning you learn that one of your buddies came in short, landed on the wrong side of the fence, hit the fence and then the throttle. Took off with barbed wire streaming back, flew the full pattern, landed and was told he was through flying. Two years in the program, then washout. Could have been worse.

The Pea Patch

The briefing was simple: "Your final flight test will be to make six landings in the "Pea Patch." There will be 12 gliders in the formation. You will do a 180-degree landing from an altitude of three hundred feet. The final approach is over a field of stumps. Four hundred feet from the edge of the stumps will be a row of fifteen-foot trees set in pipes in the ground. You will stop, in formation, before the trees. The success of this maneuver will depend on the proper execution of your flight patterns. Any questions?"

I heard a mumbled, "I hate that word execution!"

"Flight A will take off at 0800 hours."

I was in flight A. Our aircraft was the CG4A combat glider. Forty eight feet long, with a wingspan of 83 feet, that carried, besides the pilot and co-pilot, 13 fully equipped combat troops, or a jeep, a 75 pack Howitzer cannon, or a jeep trailer with a liaison radio, etc. During training our cargo was sandbags. A C47 aircraft using a nylon rope towed the glider. On landing you immediately dumped the aircraft on its reinforced nose and skidded to a stop in a very short distance. You could then raise the entire nose section and unload the jeep or whatever other cargo you carried. Our ultimate mission was to land and deliver men and materiel behind enemy lines.

We took off at 0800 hours. Six tugs, each towing two gliders. I was number six. I cut on the downwind leg, turned onto the base, then final approach. The guys ahead of me were flying a good pattern so I came in over the stumps, touched down with brakes full on, dumped it on its nose and skidded (stinkbug style) up to the glider before the trees. By the time I climbed out, all twelve gliders were down. One tail assembly wiped out by the guy behind was the only damage. There was no real order to the formation.

My second flight was not as successful for the group. Two gliders collided on the ground and were badly damaged. No one was hurt.

By the third flight everyone was getting a little jumpy. We were aware of the many things that could go wrong. It was necessary that everyone fly an exact pattern at the proper speed and altitude during the descent. If you fouled up, the guys behind you were forced into a "Every man for himself" situation. There was no motor and propeller to let us go around again. I came in behind a guy who was too high. He pulled it up into a stall, dropped about twenty-five feet. The right wheel come off and bounded up through the wing. Wingtips slammed to the ground. I was far enough behind to get down OK.

My fifth flight was a "Buddy Ride." That meant that you could chose your co-pilot. Jack asked me to ride with him, so I did. When we were coming in over the stumps, at about forty feet, the right wing dropped and Jack couldn't get it to come up. He had been fighting it for several seconds, it would not respond. Suddenly he threw up his hands, looked at me and said, "Isn't that the damnest thing you ever saw?"

I grabbed the wheel, cranked it far over to the left. The wing came up and we landed, all in about two seconds. We later figured that the wing had been in the wing wash of the preceding glider and that ground effect, actually caused the wing to lift.

A flight got in all the required landings in the twelve-glider formation. No other flight did. The wear and tear on nerves and gliders proved too costly.

By the time flights G and H came along, they were down to two gliders at a time. Nerves were so shot that, in one instance, we saw the No. 1 glider, on a tow, hang on far too long, then cut, and continue on his downwind leg. Finally he turned onto the base leg. Realizing he was too far away, he whipped into the final approach, only to disappear behind a barn, a half-mile away. We hopped into a jeep and went down there. Sure enough, he was parked in the farmers yard, the glider undamaged.

The last flight into the "Pea Patch," we witnessed, was a single Glider. He was so shook that he touched down in the first part of the patch, never dumped the Glider on its nose, went rolling past where the trees used to be, then out into the stumps, completely trashing the Glider.

We survivors decided that formation landing of the CG4A was a flawed concept. Consider this, you are at the controls of this very large aircraft, weighing up to four tons, falling out of the sky at over sixty miles per hour, with three minutes or less to determine the start and length of the three legs of your approach, correct your path in accordance with the actions of the gliders ahead, land (at sixty miles an hour you would use up your four hundred feet in eight seconds) and avoid crashing into another craft.

Something like this, "I cut, tap the airspeed, (it was stuck). That's better. Focus on my landing spot. I'm too high! Make a slipping turn. That's good! It's a mess down there. My spots gone! What's he doin'? Damn! I have to go around him. Drop the nose. Altitude for distance. Almost scraping the stumps. Pull up. Jam on the brakes, HARD. We hit the dirt. DUMP HER! DAMN! We did it! We stop. Tail falls back down."

"WE'VE GRADUATED!"

"Was it just an exercise in controlling fear? Was it worth dozens of damaged gliders, many injuries, but, thankfully, no deaths?"

Ted

Ted and I were tent mates in France. Pulled the WWII Airborne Mission across the Rhine, into Germany, as Glider Pilots. He was presumed dead but showed up six weeks later. We talked.

He said "I saw the flare and cut from the tug. Saw you cut loose at the same time."

"Yeah! Damned anti-aircraft was playing a tune on the tubing soon as I cut. Looked ahead and saw gliders being blown out of the sky. Too damn high. We were at fifteen hundred feet, 'stead of 300!"

"You sure went into a helluva dive. I followed you down."

"Well, I saw that railroad on a fill. It was a lot higher than the field. Figured to get down behind it so they couldn't hit me. Turned right then gave the controls to Herbie my co-pilot. He could see what was comin' up behind while we did the 180 turn."

"I was on your tail when we were hit. Martin, my co-pilot, slumped over and I knew he was dead. The English operator, for the liaison radio, was also killed. Right after that I was hit and my right leg and back were on fire with pain. I was going like a bat out of hell. Up ahead were all those tall trees and the farmhouse."

"Yeah, that's when I grabbed the wheel from Herbie. Airspeed was one forty. Christ! There was a road angling across the field a couple of feet high so I got right down on the deck. When I came to the road I kicked the bird into a skid, wiped out the gear. I jammed it up on the skids, slid a hundred and fifty feet and stopped."

"I know, I sailed right over you. Had to do a 90 to the right, up and over the rail embankment, slammed her down in the field between the railroad and the Germans. I guess I got out of the glider before passing out 'cause the next thing I knew a German guy was kicking me in the ribs. Several of them gathered around and were jabbering. I couldn't understand them. Then I faded again. Woke up on a cot in a bunker. Was dizzy with pain whenever I was awake. Went back to sleep."

"An Officer shook me awake. Started asking questions. I couldn't understand a word and didn't care. He finally left."

"One of the other guys brought me some sausage and potatoes. I didn't eat. The pain had me in agony. I was stiff, gawd awful sore. Weak as a cat."

"When I opened my eyes next time a guy was holding a pistol. I thought he was going to kill me. He turned the gun around and put it under my stomach. 'You kill Officer!' he said."

"Christ! I couldn't kill a fly! I couldn't even hold a gun up. He grabbed my shoulder. 'You kill Officer! We surrender to you!'"

"I can't, dammit, too weak!"

"He shook his head and went out. Me too."

"Next time I woke it was daylight. There were several Germans in the bunker. They were friendly. One took the gun. 'OKAY! No more Officer!'"

"A German medic went to work on my back. More guys came in with a stretcher."

"We carry you to Americans! We are your prisoners!"

"So that's how it was. They carried me and a whole bunch of white flags across the lines. Twenty-one of them surrendered. I went to a hospital and now I'm back."

"I'll drink to that!"

"Eh Wot?"

There was a knock on the door. I said, "Come in!" Meg entered the room carrying two towels and a wash cloth. She stopped. I had to strain back with my head to see her. Her eyes were wide with wonder, her jaw dropped. She stood, startled by the fact that I was in a handstand on the arms of the chair. My heels heavenward, where my eyes should be.

Recovering slightly she said, "I brought you some fresh towels!"

"Okay, thank you very much."

She placed the towels on the stand, then turning, opened the door. Still shocked she backed out into the hall pulling the door shut. This was England, 1945. I was an Air Corps glider pilot on detached duty, going to school in Birmingham. The war was over. Several million Americans were in Europe and the British Isles, marking time with fill in programs while awaiting the 'yearned for' ship home.

I was staying in an old Victorian Home, now a rooming house. A middle-aged couple ran it. The man, George, was Service Manager for a very large automobile dealer. His wife, Hannah ran the rooming house. Meg was a young wife who lived there with her husband, Jim. Jim spent most of his time in London so Meg was alone most of the time. She helped Hannah some, possibly to help pay the rent.

"Why was I in a handstand?"

I had been relaxing in the chair when it dawned on me that this was a beautifully made, structurally sound sitting device. Sturdy legs, substantial posts and carefully carved armrests that curved to form the back. I grabbed the armrests and lifted myself off the seat. This was great, no wiggle and no squeak. Hell, this was just like the parallel bars in a gym. Crossing my legs and tucking them tightly I pulled my bottom half through, raised it above my shoulders, unfolded my legs, straightened them out, put my feet together, pointed my toes and was in a perfectly balanced handstand. I had been there only a moment when there was the knock on the door.

I dropped out of the handstand, picked up a towel and the wash cloth and went down the hall to the bathroom.

Back in the room I heard the first bell so went down to have dinner. The residents were all gathered in the drawing room staring at Jim. He had placed a small pillow on the floor in the corner and was standing on his head, feet braced against the wall. In his hand he held a glass of beer.

At a loss I turned to George. "What's this!"

"It all started when Meg came down and told about you standing on your hands on the chair. She was excited and told everyone. Jim got ticked. The more she talked about it the angrier he became. He shouted, "I can top any damn Yank any time! Let's see him do this! I'll stand on my head and drink this glass of beer!"

The ladies were all talking to each other, overly loud, with too many gestures. An occasional quick glance to the corner then back to the chatter.

Some of the men were snickering as Jim struggled to get another gulp or two up to his stomach. His red face and the pillow were wet. A small pool had gathered.

The double bell announced dinner so the ladies moved out, followed by the men.

The old, walrus mustached gent on my right jabbed me in the ribs with his elbow, looked back at Jim, then said, "Meg has been having a go with you Yanks. That's why Jim's got his wind up. Lost cause I'd say—Eh Wot?"

Wiesbaden

The war in Europe had ended. We were on detached duty, attending schools in England. In order to get our flight time in, to receive flight pay, we would have to go back to our base in France. Four of us Glider Pilots went into the Operations Office at Bovington Air Base, near London to see if we could catch a ride to Paris.

The Air Force had converted the Troop Carrier Command into an Airline. Most of the travelers were high-ranking officers or UNRA personnel. Fortunately for us they were using Glider Pilots as dispatchers. We checked with the Glider Pilot dispatcher. No room! The plane was loaded with brass. "Hang tough a while, 'til the pilot gets here. He's a real hot rock. Might take you!"

When the flight crew arrived, were briefed and the flight plan was approved, the pilot was told of our need. "Hell yes! You guys walk out with us. You all get in the pilothouse. Just duck way down when we taxi up by the tower and stay down 'til we are loaded and on our way. You stay up front for takeoff and when get to altitude, and I've got her trimmed out, then you can go back and sit down.

We followed instructions. The pilot, co-pilot, crew chief and the four of us were jammed into the tiny pilothouse. Fifteen minutes into the flight the pilot said, "Move out!" I squeezed through the door, ignored the stares from the passengers facing each other on bench seats, and sat down in the aisle, at their feet. As I got settled I looked up to see Milt easing through the door. We were all wearing Class A uniforms, with prominent wings on the blouse. Anxiety was now in evidence in the passengers as there were now two pilots sitting in the aisle.

Bob popped out with a big smile and joined us on the floor.

A colonel, up front near the door, was getting restless and irritated. His face and neck were red. He could not remain still. Just then Cacy slipped out. The colonel jumped to his feet, shouldered Cacy into the passengers on the other side, flung open the cockpit door. Serenely shepherding the C47 through the skies was the Pilot, Co-Pilot and the Crew Chief. All was calm in the heavens.

At Paris we had learned that our squadron had transferred to Germany. (Volunteered by our Colonel, for occupation duty.) We inquired about getting to Wiesbaden and was told, "See that C47 loading up out there? It's going to Wiesbaden!"

Chase and I ran out on the apron, up the steps and were stopped by the crew chief. "What do you want?" he asked.

"We're going to Wiesbaden!"

"We're already full!"

Well, Bob told him, "We're supposed to be on this flight!"

"What are your names?"

"Chase and Conover!" He looked at the manifest.

"You're not on here, you'll have to get off!"

Just then a bellow came from the pilot. "What the hell's holding us up? Close the goddam door!"

"Yes Sir! We stepped aside, he closed the door, and we took our seats on the floor and were on our way to Wiesbaden and a new dilemma.

When we arrived we located our outfit in a small hotel they had taken over. Our buddies welcomed us. Because there was no duty, the war was over, we had a perpetual party. After a week of this it was getting old and, in our sober moments, we began to worry about getting back to England. Then we ran into the Englishmen. They were the pilots on a military airline the British had set up. Because the British were the best in the world in the use of the new fangled Radar they were pioneering the concept of all weather flying. They were the only service, Wiesbaden to London. Our boys were grounded until the weather improved.

There was a big party going on in the hotel. We were pretty well loaded when we got hungry. One of our old tentmates in France, Ted, had a well-stocked larder of goodies, sent over by his loving sisters. He invited the English blokes and us up to his room to have a midnight repast. Because England had been on short rations for several years, the cookies, cheeses, jams and other goodies, provided by Ted, sent our English friends into ecstatic rapture. They were extremely grateful.

During this time we let it be known that Chase and I should get back to England. "No problem, chaps, just drop into the OP's office at 0500 hours in the morning and we will escort you to jolly old London town!"

Chase and I showed up at the appointed hour, bleary eyed and boozy. We really didn't know what to expect, didn't believe they would really remember, but felt it was worth a chance. Walking in the door we saw, maybe, fifty or so officers sitting in the waiting room. Most of them were Colonels or high UNRA officials. A few others, maybe Majors, had managed to qualify.

We stood there, lowly Flight Officers, wondering what the hell we were doing there when the door to the operations office abruptly opened and one of our English friends emerged, arms wide, a big smile.

"Good morning. Come in here!" he beckoned.

We followed him into the operations office, followed by the eyes of a very exalted and interested audience. As there was a large plate glass window separating the two rooms, everyone saw the Lieutenant pick up the manifest, scratch off the last two names. He added our names, entered them on the manifest, shook our hands then escorted us back to the waiting room.

"It will be just a few minutes," he said.

Soon the flight was announced. "Colonel Parks, Colonel

Waters, Colonel Carter, etc. The last two names were Flight Officer Chase and Flight Officer Conover. We arose and followed our distinguished companions aboard the aircraft. The witnesses sat stunned. Grounded by the fog and the whimsies of fate for yet another day or week.

We broke through the fog at 100 feet having been on instruments all the way, landed and debarked at Bovington Airfield, London.

"We were AWOL, Right! We had no passport! Right! We had to go through customs! Right?"

Chase and I followed the other passengers into the terminal. The line extended across a large general office, along a low fence-like partition. Ahead we could see the customs agent checking passports. Chase and I stepped over the fence, wandered casually, through the office, smiled and nodded at the clerks, bypassed the customs agent and joined a line where we converted our German marks to English currency.

Moral: "Always remember, when your heart is pure, Good Things Happen!"

Tidworth

The big news was: Military personnel presently in England, who had sufficient Service Points could ship out from there instead of going back to their units on the Continent. The problem was that I would not have enough points until 10 days after my school session ended.

I had been on Detached Duty, in Birmingham, on an Information and Education program. It was a "Something to Do" device to relieve the boredom of waiting to ship out to the states for discharge. Now, if I went back to Germany I would be on Occupation Duty and could be there a year or more. The war had ended. As far as I was concerned the soldiering part of my life was over. FINI! As the French say.

I was in the bar at the Officers Club. Next to me was a Colonel in the Medical Corp. We chatted a while, usual stuff— "Where you from? How long have you been in?" Etc. I told him of my problem.

"I can help solve that for you son. I'm running a Dental Clinic in Halesford. When your school session ends come on down and I will check you into the clinic. You can stay there until your point total is up."

I bought him a drink, got the address and hoped for the best.

The day I was supposed to return to Germany I hopped the two-story bus. After stopping every mile or so, the five-hour journey ended. I found the Clinic. Low and behold, the Colonel remembered.

He examined my teeth, had a nice room, with an outside entrance assigned to me, said I should come back on the proper day for my discharge papers, from the Clinic.

On the magic day I checked out and took the train for London. I found the Headquarters of the Commanding General, American Forces for the British Isles. The Warrant Officer at the desk said, "Hi! Buddy, what can I do for you?" The fact that I was also a Warrant Officer paved the way.

"You can send me home!" I handed him my papers.

"Hmm! See what I can do." I waited. "Here we go. I'll transfer you to an Artillery unit, stationed at Tidworth. They will be shipping out from Southampton in six weeks. OK?"

"Yes! Yes! That's wonderful."

Tidworth was a holdover installation from World War I. The Artillery unit was running it temporarily. Major O'Neal listened to my story then made me "Utilities Officer" for the base. He gave me a jeep and told me I was in charge of all utilities such as the carpenter shop, plumbing shop, electrical, heating, telephone, etc. I had to sign for nearly a half million dollars worth of material. I was stunned but said, "Thank You!" and left. I spent the time visiting with the guys in the shops. Never issued an order.

Tidworth was processing one thousand GI brides for shipment to the States. Most of the barracks were empty except for a small cadre of British soldiers. My squadron had finally traced me by the time the six weeks were up. Major O'Neal never answered any of the TWX inquiries, according to Lt. Boyle, his adjutant.

We left Southampton on a Victory Ship. After an eleven-day sail on the edge of a violent storm we arrived in the homeland. I was on my way to a court marshal or a discharge. Time would tell.

Statue of Liberty

The Statue of Liberty means something to me. I have seen it twice and each time was under gut wrenching circumstances.

In February, 1945—wartime— a black drizzly night on a New York dock, 10,000 troops filed slowly forward under a sparse string of lights past the Red Cross coffee stands to board the liner "Ill de France." Burdened by full pack and more heavily by our thoughts the other Glider Pilots and I waited for the ordeal to end. Finally we were aboard, had stowed our gear in the 18 inch by 30 inch by eight foot bunk space which was our very own.

I shoved, squeezed and elbowed my way out of the quarters and onto the darkened deck to watch our departure. It was past midnight. The few lights in use stabbed from the dark like flashes of white fire. Now we were moving out into black enveloping night and someone set our course toward the unknown. Behind us we watched as America withdrew. Sound, light and silhouette were replaced by the feel, smell and the chunking sound of a ship under way.

"There she is!" someone pointed. Others joined. "There she is over there!"

Her torch, held high, flared brilliantly. The light from her base softly bathed the full dimensional, jewel-like figure set on a rich black velvet background. I watched her gradually diminish and finally disappear from view. The final clinging bit of the old everyday life was extracted and I had left America. The unlighted, rolling ship surged forward on and on into the stygian mantle of night.

War is a personal experience. No two people can agree on,

exactly, what it is like. It is a fabric woven with the life threads of wives, mothers, children, with the soldier shuttles working through the woofs of uncounted acts of bravery, compassion, stupidity, brutality, and competence, moving on to complete a shroud for mankind.

In my case I had advanced to the objective, "Luck" when the war ended. Suddenly, I looked around and the world was bright. The future promising. Nineteen million other guys and gals and I were instant civilians. Still in uniform but aware that we were on borrowed time and eager to get back and pick up the good, no, the great old half-forgotten life. I finally got on a Victory ship, (Ha! "VICTORY") and lived and lounged my way across the wild, stormy Atlantic to good old New York.

When we sailed into the harbor there she was—The Lady of Liberty—waiting in the beautiful sunlight, with the magnificent skyline, solid, immense and reassuring, behind her.

"Damn, damn, ain't she something. Really nice!"

"OH! YOU BEAUTIFUL DOLL!"

House

To have a home you first must obtain, build or inherit a house. Ours was built and I can tell you, that wasn't easy. Besides a hammer, saw, square, etc., a very useful thing in that endeavor is money. Not just some, but lots and lots of the stuff.

When I came back to Alaska after the War (WWII) it was with the promise to Bobbie that we would return to Anchorage where we had a residential lot, build a house and then, in five years sell it and return to the States. I made that promise. It was, actually, forty-five years before we returned to her birthplace in Washington State.

A whole bunch of things happened in that time, including building two houses, raising four children, operations for my wife Bobbie, homesteading, half a dozen different occupations, then, finally, fulfilling my promise to return to the states.

We had managed to save two thousand dollars during the four and a half years I was in the Air Corps. Bobbie and our oldest son, Dale, barely getting by while waiting for Daddy, only accomplished this. Her parents and mine had helped when they could.

Now we were back. I rented a bulldozer, dug the hole for the basement, bought some 2x8, 2x4, 1x8 shiplap lumber, nails etc. and started the project. I had a hammer, a combination rip and crosscut saw (I couldn't afford one of each) a square, and a whole bunch of ignorance about the art of carpentry. The house was rectangular so I didn't have to worry about jogs, etc. I just leveled for the footings, then built the forms for the concrete footings and walls. This was before the common use of plywood so I used 1x8 shiplap. This, of course, required a lot more labor than would be necessary now.

When I had all the outside walls, of the forms, raised, I had to mark the level for the top of the future concrete wall. I couldn't afford a transit and had never heard of a water level. So put a pole up in the center of the site, took my level and taped it to a sixteen foot 2x4, set one end on the pole and marked the wall at the other end when it read level. Figured I had a constant error so it would work. I snapped a line from mark to mark, nailed on a strip of quarter round and was all set.

To get the proper thickness for the concrete I used one-inch square sticks, 8 inches long. These spaced the inner and outer walls. Wire was then wrapped around the horizontal walers, twisted to hold the ends of the spacers, tightly, against the inner and outer forms. One way to break wire is to twist it so the nightmare of this part of the construction was "Did I twist it enough? Too much? If one breaks will the rest go pop! Pop! Pop! Until the concrete is a huge hardening pile where the basement should be?"

This is a lot of talk about the first step but does point out the truth of the saying, "There is nothing more terrifying than ignorance in action." Really tells it all.

It was the middle of October by the time we were ready for the concrete. They would quit delivering concrete if the temperature dropped any more, so with frantic effort I finished and called for the mix.

So there we were, pregnant Bobbie and I and a huge truck full of heavy concrete. The truck could only reach one corner of the forms. He added extra water to the mix so we could puddle it down the forms with short lengths of 2x4s. We had to go under the window forms, get it to the corners each way. It was a tremendous job with the guy going back for more three times. Total 24 cubic yards of concrete. A cubic yard is 3ft by 3ft by 3ft. Twenty-four of these in a column would tower 72 feet in the air. Twenty-four yards at forty two hundred pounds each totals 302,400 pounds. My poor pregnant Bobbie was doing all she could to help.

I have had many people tell me the smartest thing I ever did was to marry Bobbie. Funny I've never heard anyone say, "Bobbie, the smartest thing you ever did— (should end with Don) (never has).

We got the damn thing poured. Winter came, I ordered 2x12x16s for the floor joists, but because of the shortage of lumber, after the war, never got them until the following April.

After I had stripped the forms I was standing back in the yard. I could see that the top of the concrete was level with the tide line, three miles away across Knik Arm of the Cook Inlet. VICTORY! That's a first class water level!

The next step in this exciting endeavor was to scrape all the concrete off the shiplap, then set the floor joist, put down the sub-floor, then frame the building. All this time we were living in my parent's house. They were in the states and I was working, part time for my brother Dean.

Bobbie's Mother and Father came up for a visit. Charlie was an excellent carpenter. He introduced me to Six, Eight, Ten. This is a magical formula that allows you to make a square corner. If you measure six feet from the corner, eight feet the other way, the distance between the marks, diagonally, will be ten feet. The corner will be perfectly square. "My God! Who ever came up with that?"

By a coincidence, fifty years later, the buyer of our home put in new kitchen cabinets. Our son Robert was in charge of the cabinet department at Eagle hardware. The sales lady that went out to measure for the new cabinets told Bob that our old house was the only square house she had ever measured. Salute to Charlie, and maybe me.

I put down the floor joist, put on the sub-floor, framed the walls, put the roof trusses in place, covered the whole thing with shiplap, and then waited to accumulate money for the roof shingles. Finally the day arrived when I could order the roof.

Bobbie's dad was desperately ill. Would die within days. Bobbie took Bob, our newborn and the money for the roof to go see her dad. She was able to be with him before he passed away.

Meanwhile I went to Columbia Lumber and told Red that I could not pay for a roof at that time. "Pay when you can." He sent the material out and I was transformed into a roofer. Shingled the damn thing myself.

Now we had a house with no windows, no doors, siding or anything else. Bobbie came back after her dad passed away. We struggled 'til we had the shingles paid for.

I put up the electrical service box and we finally had electricity. More time and scrimping and we were able to get the sewer and water lines run in. Now I had to become an electrician, then a plumber.

At that time I had to run the sewer line in from the alley. I was able to use Orangeburg plastic pipe, which was easier to install than cast iron, which had to be caulked with okum and then sealed with hot lead. The only critical item was to be sure that the fall in the line was exactly one-fourth inch to the foot. Once you got to the alley the City would make the hookup. When this was all completed we could install the shower and toilet in the basement. See what I mean about things eating up your time for living the good life.

We were still living in my Dad's house so were depriving them of rental income. When we were able to get a metal shower stall, a toilet and a pot bellied stove we moved in. OH! Yes, we had the concrete floor placed and finished by a professional. He left the surface with a rough finish so it would hold the future asphalt tile better. I still get chills down my spine when I think of our son Robert crawling, bare legged, around on that terrible concrete floor.

We had an electric light bulb on a twenty five-foot drop cord that we took from room to room. A hunk of canvas was hung for our back door. The bathroom door was there, but wasn't hung. We had a hot plate and sink, and sat on a trunk with a piece of plywood on two sawhorses for a table. What you do is make do. What made this tolerable was that veterans all around me were doing the same thing. If I ran into a problem as to how to build or fix something, I could hop in the car, check around and I would find a house that had solved that dilemma. "Ah! That's how it's done." All this time I could have been drawing down top wages as a heavy equipment operator, but I would be out in the sticks for six or seven months at a time.

Floor Tile

We ordered our floor tile from Sears. It was a dark brown with lighter flecks in it. Bobbie had designed a pattern for the center of the floor, using tan tile. Another skill, tile laying, of course required background knowledge. I read the instructions. "In order for the tile to have the best possible opportunity to bond firmly to the base, the whole area should be tiled in one session. (The tile will not bond to dry adhesive.)

The room was 14 by 20 feet plus the bathroom/bedroom hallway. If you calculate that in square footage, it comes close to 300 square feet. Using 9 by 9 inch tile means that you have over 500 tiles to firmly bond to the base once you start by laying your, first ever, asphalt tile. Once again, divorce and flee or do it.

The first thing, of course, is to snap a chalk line both ways to determine the exact center of the area. This gives you a precise point to layout the pattern. Next you carefully apply the adhesive with the notched trowel so that the pretty little ridges, in the graceful little swirls of adhesive are uniform, with no lumps here and there to squish through the joints. It is at this time that you learn you have covered up the chalk line, which was to get the project off to a proper start. The solution to this dilemma is obvious so I won't dwell on it. ("Look, I'll be eighty-two next month. How the hell can I remember all the fine details?")

The laying of the tile proceeded to the point of exhaustion, at which time I had to cut all the small pieces to bring it within 1/4 inch of the wall. The base molding would then cover the crack if we could ever afford base molding. Bobbie was there firmly pressing each tile down and wiping up any adhesive that showed on the surface.

The next day Bob had a great time sliding around on the new, clean tile floor.

Bobbie and I decided that this called for a celebration, a party. We scraped up enough for a quart of Jim Beam, invited some friends to come over later. I went to the liquor store and got the jug. Coming in the back tent flap door I was passed by the neighbor's big black Labrador running in and down the stairs. I followed and when I came into the room the son of a bitch jumped up on me, knocking the bottle out of my hand and shattering it on the new tile floor. I couldn't catch him to kill him.

Ray

"You want to what?"

"Snare a bear. I figure if we go down to McNeil River and set up a platform in a tree, then snare a Brownie, shoot him with my camera, we'll have one hell of a movie!"

To myself, "Is this guy tired of living?"

Ray and I had been neighbors ever since I had come back from the war. That is after I had made my house somewhat livable and moved the family in. Fact is—I had bought my lot from Ray before the war when he had subdivided his mink ranch. We were on the Park Strip, right in the middle of Anchorage.

Ray was in his late sixties by then but was one of the Gang. The rest of us were in our thirties, most of us building our own houses. There were 18 houses completed within sight of mine before I got it far enough along to move the family in. Even then, it was primitive living.

Ray had been an Engineer on the Alaska Railroad. He had been married, in the States, but for several years was a swinging bachelor.

When he was fifty-five, on a dare at a wild party, he had jumped into Lake Spenard from the Idle Hour dock. The ice had been out, maybe a week. They fished him out, took him home, undressed him, put him to bed and left, figuring he had passed out. Two days later someone checked on him. He was still lying in bed. At the hospital they said that he had suffered a major stroke. Ray recovered his spirit but not his physical faculties. His left foot dragged when he walked and he could not raise his left arm. With practically no help, he had built a two story duplex, even though, in order to drive a nail he would have to put the nail in his left hand, raise that arm with his right to the proper position, then grab the hammer and drive the nail. He had the patience and the independence to make it work. When he had completed that Duplex he converted his cold storage locker, from his mink ranching days into another duplex.

While I had been away in the service, my brother, Dean, and Ray had done a lot of hunting, trapping and fishing together. Ray could do just about anything in the woods, even handle snowshoes, if someone broke trail in the light stuff. They always came home with game—moose, caribou, fish, beaver, or whatever they went after. When I came back Ray dropped out and Dean and I hunted together.

With his pension from the railroad, his income from three apartments, Ray was far better off financially than any of us.

I asked Ray one day, "How do you accomplish so much?"

"I never had anything until I quit chasing women. On the buildings I just make sure that I get something done every day. It adds up."

Ray had a nice car, good clothes, and no desires whatever to go outside (to the lower 48 states). He bought an airplane and was learning to fly. He had soloed then gave up the piloting and depended on his friends to fly him around. I took him wolf hunting a couple of times. There was a $50 bounty on wolves. Pretty good money. What made this wolf hunting a very questionable enterprise, indeed, was the fact that Ray could not hold a shotgun steady enough to aim and shoot because of the bad left arm. He had to swing the gun and, at the proper time, pull the trigger.

His airplane was a J3 Cub with a side door that swung half up and half down. The procedure was to come up behind the running wolf, 15 or 20 feet above him, then at the proper instant, kick the airplane into a skid. Now you're flying sort of sideways. This maneuver is something you had trained for years, not to do at all when close to the ground.

Now the shooter lines up on the wolf and shoots just behind it.

The speed of the airplane picks up the difference and you've got a wolf, maybe! One major complication to this is that the strut, going from the lower fuselage to the wing is the only reason that wing stays where it is. This strut is also directly in the line of fire. Hopefully, if things work out right the shooter misses the strut and hits the wolf. This whole experience is extended pucker time. And the fact that Ray is taking a swing shot, it has even less appeal. I had been a combat Glider Pilot during World War II so wasn't actively seeking any new thrills. Twice was enough for the wolf hunting.

Ray was of average height, billiard ball bald, had a smooth, pink Scandinavian face and happy, baby blue eyes, and a beautiful smile. Our wives were all pretty women who fussed over Ray. His grin told us he loved it. Ray was always a gentleman toward our gals. My wife, Bobbie, made special cakes for his birthdays. They always had a distinct motif tied to one of Ray's activities, wolf, airplanes, trapping, etc. We'd always throw a big party and present the cake, but he would never let us eat it. At one time he had six cakes sitting on his mantel.

These were lean times for Bobbie, the kids and I. I was trying to change my occupation, stay in town with the family instead of running a dozer in some God forsaken spot in the interior of Alaska. We raised our kids on moose and caribou. When I was finally able to buy some beef roast the kids thought there was something wrong with the meat. Once in a while Ray would show up with a sack of groceries, then just leave it when he left.

Ray never did find anyone to share his enthusiasm for the grabbing of a 1500-pound Brownie. Seems like all us pilots had other priorities and just didn't get around to it.

Ray got cancer. His long time renters and friends, Jack and Norma took care of him. Ray wouldn't see any of the rest of us. We took stuff over to him but never got a chance to say "Good Bye." He gave one of his duplexes to Jack and Norma. Some relation came up from the states, sold the other duplex, and junked all of Ray's wonderful wildlife pictures and personal possessions. Ray was a good friend, a very memorable man.

Stucco

I finally got a job delivering magazines and we had a steady income. When we started our family I insisted and Bobbie agreed that she would stay home and raise the family. This she did 'til Russell, the youngest, was in high school. I appreciate that very much.

We gradually got a back door, other doors, light fixtures, an electric stove etc. It was several years before we were able to get a refrigerator. We had a screened cooler hanging just outside the window.

Now the shiplap was curling. It was so bad that siding could not be applied and have a nice finish. We discussed it and finally decided that stucco was the most practical solution, even though there were no windows.

Another challenge. My father's living room was plastered and the old guy who had done it was an excellent artisan. Beautiful job. I asked him if he would stucco our house. He agreed and told me to get some 15 pound felt paper, staple that on the house, then apply chicken wire with Stucco nails. These hold the chicken wire about a 3/8-inch away from the shiplap, and reinforced the stucco. I was finally able to get it ready and searched out himself. Found him sitting on a bench in the sun with some of his old buddies downtown by Gil's Garage on Fourth Avenue.

"Mr. Cook, I've got my house ready for the stucco. Could you come and finish the job?"

"Oh yes, well, you're younger than I am. You do it."

"But you promised me! You said you'd do it!"

"Look, I'm seventy two. I think you should do it."

"But I don't know how.

"You know what a hawk and a trowel are?"

"Yes, I've seen them used."

"OK. Mix three sand to one Masonry Cement and have at it." He turned back to his buddies.

Dad agreed to mix the mud for me. I climbed the scaffold I had prepared, hoisted up a bucket of mix and embarked on another thrilling experience in the art of home building. I should tell you that a hawk is a sixteen-inch square aluminum plate with a one and one half, by seven-inch handle riveted to the center. You know what a plaster trowel looks like. I put a gob of mix on the hawk, held it front of me, tilted it and transferred some of it to the trowel with an up and away motion of my right arm. This was successful in loading the trowel but dumped the balance from the hawk onto my stomach and down my legs. I reached as high as I could and pushed some of the mix through the screen, the rest falling to the ground far below. I became instantly aware that there was something wrong with my technique. Most of the mix should be pressed into the stucco wire with only a negligible amount going as waste. Dad said nothing, but moved farther away from the scene. I tried again, same results. "Maybe if I did it a little faster!" Didn't work. Slower, same result. Have a cigarette; think it over! Did nothing. Dad and I worked the afternoon away, stuccoed me, the scaffold, a large portion of the ground, and finally called it a day. I had less than two feet down from the gable peak stuccoed. Something like this bruises a guy's feeling of invincibility.

Enter salvation. The next day I went a block or so to where Mack Mortensen, a plastering contractor, was stuccoing his duplex. I didn't want to show my ignorance so just watched him. Finally I noticed that when he filled his hawk with mud he would wipe the top of the heap with his trowel. This of course forced the air out from under the gob on the hawk and made it stick. I got Dad and we went to work again. Low and behold, it worked. From then on we worked as a team and we did the whole last wall of the building in one day. Because you push up and away with the trowel the muscles in your shoulder, never used before in this manner, develop a resentment toward you that continues for a very long and painful period, say three or four months.

Now I found out that I was eligible for the Alaska Territorial Veterans loan. This was a $10,000 loan from the Government for use to build a home or start a business. I could obtain lumber, plumbing, electrical materials and when I had built it in or installed it they would inspect it, approve it and then make a check payable to me and the supplier. I would sign it, give it to the vendor and was then eligible for another batch of dough. What a godsend. It was a revolving fund that was so successful that only 2% was lost throughout the whole program. It gave two or three hundred vets a needed leg up on the ladder.

One thing they required to qualify was a blueprint of the house. We didn't have a blueprint and I sure as hell knew nothing about making one. I decided I would make a model. This I did, even had a removable roof and top floor so that they could see everything. Some jawing back and forth but they finally said OK and we were in.

I mentioned before that ignorance was one of the tools I brought to this endeavor. For example, I didn't know that it took 1000 man-hours for skilled craftsmen to complete an average house at that time. That is four months of continuous eight-hour days. If you can only work an hour of two in the evening, this extends the completion to the far distant future. I mentioned skilled craftsmen. That means that there are men skilled in several different crafts, such as carpentry, plumbing, electrical, painting, paper hanging, tile setting, carpet laying, and forty seven other skills. Each of these artisans have spent years learning what you must do from scratch well enough so that your wife will still speak to you and not withhold favors.

Another little item to ponder is that there were, at that time, at least seventeen separate operations to complete an outside wall. You have the inside finish, the wallboard, the spackling, the vapor barrier, the insulation, the studs, etc, etc, etc. With no electric chop saws, staplers, nailers, and other labor saving devices, you can see that it is a tremendously tedious task. I started to calculate how many times my right arm moved with that sad sack saw I was stuck with. The more I calculated the closer I came to crying so I quit.

Now that the building was stuccoed we became eligible to get some windows. I'm sure the neighbors were happy about that. No longer would they have to look at a bare stuccoed building with black tarpaper showing at the openings in the stucco left for the windows. Among the windows were three four foot by five foot, by one-inch Thermopane units. Two would be installed in front and one around the corner of the living room. The two, installed together, would require an opening over eight feet wide. This meant a truss had to span the distance and be strong enough to support the roof and a snow load of maybe three or four feet. I carefully constructed the truss, cut the opening and installed the millwork. The long awaited time had come.

We were excited that we would have the expected view of Mt McKinley right there. Problem was the damn windows were warped. Thermopane Windows made of 1/4-inch plate glass with a one half-inch lead spacer between them at the edges. This gave the needed insulation value to the outside wall. Trouble was, these windows were warped and could not be installed properly. One bottom corner on each was nearly two inches out. Tragedy!

I called Glass Sash and Door. They told me that the Thermopane man was there and I could see him. I rushed down and told him my problem.

"No sweat! Just lay them flat for three or four days. You must have had them leaned, improperly, against the wall for a long time.

I did as he suggested and in a few days they were back to normal and installed beautifully. Lesson number 261 on home building. The rest of the windows were double hung with storm sash so were no trouble to install, except, the bathroom where we had decided to use glass block.

Ever watch a block layer? They grab a block, load the trowel with mortar, wipe the ends leaving just the right amount on the two extrusions at each end, drop it in the bed of mortar, tap it gently in place, scrape the excess from the joints and reach for another block. What I have just described is not possible for a normal human being, like you or me. My task was to install the glass block four wide and six high in the window opening. It should become a symmetrical, stable unit. I found that each block had its own preference for position and seemed to resent my attempt to give them all the same, uniform appearance. Some wanted to tilt, others to lean or squish out the bed of mortar. It's hard to be in a situation where you can't discuss the problem. Glass blocks are really dumb!

Gypsum is a white kind of rock. Plasterboard is called Sheetrock. This is a wonderful fire retardant wall paneling that comes in 4x8 by 1/2-inch sheets. Because it is rock it is—You guessed it, heavy. I mean **very heavy**! Picture me with one of these monster sheets resting on my head and shoulders, fumbling for a nail or two so I can transfer the burden to the ceiling where it rightfully belongs. This practice results in countless misplaced vertebrae, ruptures, hernia sprains, divorces and other painful ends. I'm sure there are countless tricks that simplify installation of this product. I am also sure that I avoided all of them.

Taping is something else. After a while you become proud of the beautiful smooth job you think you have, at last, been able to do.

Looks great, you paint it. Your wife says, "How come there are those creases and streaks there, Honey?" No, I will not use an obscenity.

Plumbing

"Why Don, are you building such a big house?"

At that time most of the houses in Anchorage had been built in the twenties or before. They were small, snug, cheap to heat and simple to maintain. I thought of that question, many times when I fumbled through the ordeal of plumbing for two kitchens, two bathrooms, a utility room and of course the outside faucets.

All water lines were then run in galvanized iron pipe. This meant scores of cut and thread joints. There were no plastic or copper supply lines in those days. A threaded joint requires careful measurement of the pipe so that the joint will be water tight when tightened. The waste lines were cast iron so required that Okum rope be tamped down in the joint, then covered with molten lead to make the seal. All this was incredibly time consuming when approached with ignorance and no experience. Eventually it was a workable system that never gave a problem. Something right?

The electrical system was not a problem. Just took a lot of time.

Heating

When I became eligible for the Vets loan we contracted to have a hot water heating system installed. This too was beyond my experience.

The contractor was a friend of my Dad. They had worked together at Fort Richardson. This fellow then started up his heating business. Dad said he was OK so I gave him free rein. The result was a minimum installation at maximum price. Really stabbed me he did, I learned later.

Now we had heat throughout the house, it could be regulated, and did not require cutting and chopping wood. Just a switch. Lasted for twenty years and then I changed it all. Had some money by that time.

Eventually I got a much better job, utilizing my sales experience. As our income increased we remodeled the home, added a fireplace, new cabinets, appliances, new paneling and a new entrance.

We now had four children, Dale, Robert, Patrecia, and Russell. Patrecia was born on my birthday. That's another story.

We had accumulated a small cabin cruiser, an airplane, and two commercial properties. Living pretty well. Time for a change.

Homestead

"And thank you, God, for our homestead," Our youngest son, Russell, proclaimed as he concluded grace one evening.

Startled, my wife questioned, "What homestead?"

Russell piped up, "The homestead we're going to get."

My wife looked at me. "What is this all about?"

Well, I said, "We were going to look at a homestead."

We, the children and I, had been out to our rental building, painting and preparing it for a new tenant when we decided to go out for hamburgers. Joe, a former work associate, entered the restaurant. He had to leave employment at Anchorage Sand and Gravel because of a bad heart. And had found a new occupation. This was researching the homesteads around Anchorage and Wasilla to find out what was available and open to entry, what might be challenged, and those that had been abandoned. He came over to the table.

"Don," he said, "I've got just the homestead for you! It's near Wasilla, it nearly surrounds one lake and it corners in another." He spread out a chart from the Bureau of Land Management. It showed an inked in square. Pointing to it Joe said, "This has been abandoned by the original homesteader. You see, Don, this is a quarter section of land that's 160 acres, only a little over two miles from Big Lake. It nearly surrounds one lake and corners in another. A nice, nice piece of property." He offered to help us file on it. He knew all the ropes. For a fee of two hundred dollars he would furnish us with the information necessary and assist us in the formal homestead application. I told him that I would consider it and take the boys and have a look at the property. If we were interested I would contact him and further the deal.

There had been a rush to homestead around that time. There really wasn't any very good land available that was close enough and accessible for non-hermits to obtain. This property was sixty-five miles from Anchorage, fifteen miles from Wasilla and only two and a half miles from Big Lake, which was the biggest water recreation area in Alaska. With over seven hundred cabins on it.

We had to give him an answer as soon as possible because it was his livelihood. The following Sunday I took Bob, our twelve-year-old son, and went looking. We drove up to a small plane airstrip near where the homestead was supposed to be, parked the car, and put on our snowshoes. I had a compass, we knew the homestead was north and east of the airstrip.

I had borrowed snowshoes for us. I had been on those hide webbed hoops before, but really wasn't the sure-footed sourdough. I was able, though, to get Bob started out OK. Being young and strong he had very little trouble. As he was much lighter in weight he didn't sink into the snow as far as old Dad so broke trail for me after he got the hang of it.

The temperature was at 30 below when we started out. We must have walked for about an hour and we couldn't find anything resembling a lake. There were smooth areas that were maybes but on further examination we found reeds and grasses that labeled it a swamp. After a long siege of damned cold wandering we still hadn't found the lake. There were no mountains visible, no landmarks that we could refer to. I had to set a course by the compass and then compensate in my head for what I thought was the deviation from the true course. Much of the time we were amid scraggly swamp spruce, and the humps and holes of that kind of country made it really tough walking. It's real easy for a novice on snowshoes to fall, but a hell of a job getting upright again. We finally concluded the search, followed our tracks back to the car and enjoyed a warm ride back to Anchorage.

A couple of weeks later, on another cold Sunday, my oldest son, Dale, joined Bob and I on another attempt. We started from the same spot and the three of us searched long and hard. Finally, Dale took off his snowshoes and climbed a spruce tree. We were in better country now, bigger spruce and some beautiful birch and aspen. He got up about twenty feet and hollered, "I think I've found it!" He came back down and we were finally headed in the right direction. Sure enough, there was the lake.

Breaking out of the trees on the south end of the lake, we walked three quarters of its length. There, on the bank, stood the ragged remnants of an old tent, the remainder of a, would be, homesteader's dream. Time and bears had shredded the evidence. A few items remained—a shovel and an ax, some cooking gear, nothing of value. We had found the homestead.

"What do you think Dad? I think it's neat!" said Dale.

"So do I. We could put a cabin right here. Right over there!" Bob pointed.

We were on a point of land near the center of the lake. I could see gravel in the bank by the tent so it would be a good building site. The cabin site would be in a grove of spruce and birch. It would sit about forty feet above lake level. The view of the Chugach mountain range and majestic Pioneer Peak would form the eastern horizon. Knock out a few trees and we would have a great view of most of the lake.

On the north side of the point we discovered a beaver lodge, occupied we knew, because of the huge feed pile of saplings and branches rising above the ice.

"Is the lake big enough for an airplane?" from Dale.

"I would say it's about a half mile, trees to trees. Big enough for a Super Cub or a One Eighty."

"Are we going to get it?" asked Bob.

"Yeah, are we?" said Dale.

"Well, we'll see. I'll have to talk to your mother, and see what she says. We'd better head back to town."

Walking by the tent on the way down the hill I wondered. "Damn, what happened."

There wasn't much talking on the walk and ride back to town. We shared a thermos of hot chocolate. Each of us was wrapped in our own fantasies of the future. In town, I called Joe and told him I was interested.

The next item of business was to talk it over with Bobbie. We had discussed the advantages of country living in raising children. Anchorage was growing rapidly so was providing options for the kids, which were not always the best for their development, too many toys and comforts. She was raised on a farm near Port Angeles, Washington, where she and her sisters had to amuse themselves with a few toys and invented games.

In 1935, when my brother Lisle, my Dad and I went to Alaska we had serious plans to consider homesteading. We didn't follow up on it. Later Bobbie and I had an opportunity to homestead just north of Lake Hood in Anchorage (now extremely valuable property) but we couldn't even afford a car to go back and forth. Hell, it was three or four miles from town. Now we decided to go ahead with this one. We thought we could afford it. Underline thought!

I called my pal Joe, the expert, and told him we wanted to go ahead with the homesteading. He helped us file. We got all the paperwork done in December of 1960, so had six months to move on the property and "prove up" as they say, so we could obtain a patent. (In homesteader lingo this means making the improvements to qualify for legal title).

For several months we made our preparations. We decided that we would build an A-frame cabin as designed by the United States Plywood Association. This would give us a loft for the kids to play and sleep in and also we would have a complete materials list to complete the cabin. This was important because all material had to go in by sled in the winter, as there was no road access to the property.

I was Sales Manager for a lumberyard so carefully selected all the materials, and built a sixteen-foot sled of four by twelve fir runners, with two-inch tongue and groove decking. We needed a tractor to pull the sled, and clear land. And build road, so I bought a John Deere 440 with an adjustable angle blade. I was assured that it was in A-one shape. It wasn't.

We hired a semi- with a forty-foot bed, loaded the cat and all the building materials and took off on the great adventure. Dale, Bob and I followed the big rig to our take-off point by the airstrip.

On arrival we had the driver back up to a berm I had spotted. This allowed us to unload the tractor. We then stacked all the lumber and materials, hooked up the sled and loaded it for the first trip into the cabin site. It's easy to stack plywood so we kept piling it on 'til we had a forty-inch load. That plus all the other materials proved too much weight. About a quarter mile down the trail, Dale was driving the cat and he went over a hump, the sled dropped a foot or so breaking the left runner about four feet from the back end. If it dropped a foot, my heart dropped about six.

"I'm real sorry Dad!" Dale said as we stood looking at the damage.

"Not you fault, son. We overloaded it and now we have to change the plan. Let's unload the sled." The three of us pitched in and soon had all the material off the sled.

"We'll cut off the other runner to the length of this one, then reload." This we did then started off again. Dale driving with more caution now. In and out, around the trees, through the willows, over the niggerheads 'til we finally broke out on the smooth snow of an ice covered lake. Then it was up and over the bank, and back into the timber. This was much more difficult. The trees were larger. They were close together creating many traps that would stop our safari if not avoided. We did have to fall some of the smaller trees, cutting them off at ground level so the sled could override their stumps. It was slow, strenuous work. I was happy and proud of my two fine boys. We finally triumphed and parked at the cabin site. Now the work could begin.

We unloaded the sled, in the cold, clear moonlight, then followed the cat and sled back, past the disaster area, to the car, parked the sled and cat by our building materials and drove back home.

The boys and I returned the next day. Two trips hauled the rest of the materials on in to the Promised Land. Hallelujah!

The next weekend the whole family walked in over the swamp. Russ at nine, his friend Mark, Pattie, our eleven-year-old girl, and, of course, Bobbie saw our future cabin site for the first time. The dogs, Pluto and Kenai, must have covered an extra twenty miles as they checked out all the great scents, burrows, and each of us, countless times. The walk in was far easier because of the trail made by the dozer tracks. This time we left the cat and sled at the cabin site.

When the weather warmed up, every weekend, we would walk in from the gravel pit on the Big Lake road where our section line intersected it. At the end of the day a tired crew would walk back out and make the sixty-mile drive back home.

When the ground thawed enough, we dug holes for the piers to support the cabin. Five gallon paint buckets served as the forms. We were lucky to have gravel on site, but we had to bring in the cement. This required land access over another person's property. We thought we had established a good relationship with one of the Homesteaders on the Big Lake Road, the one we would require permission from to bring in the cement. The man was very friendly and cooperative. He had spent several hours showing us the section line, which was our common northern boundary. Our land, however, was two miles east of his property. That was, also, when we learned that the line intersected the Big Lake Road at an altitude of a hundred feet. That fact made it impractical for us to follow the line all the way out to the road. When I sent Dale to walk the cat out so we could put the sacks of cement on the blade and carry them into the cabin we anticipated no problem. He got within about two hundred yards of the road when he had to stop, park the cat and walk out to where we were waiting.

"She won't let me bring the cat any further. She met me out in the woods, bawled me out and told me to get the damn cat off her property. Said I was knocking down all her trees. Said she wanted to talk to you, Dad!"

I knocked and she was there. I don't remember all she said. She was very insulting and had she been of the other sex would have had an altered appearance in short order. She forbade me from moving the cat, period. She said that Dale was deliberately knocking down her trees, which was utter nonsense. You always take the least troublesome way when going cross-country. I listened to the tirade for several minutes before I could reason with her. She finally relented enough to allow us to bring the cat out, get the cement and take it back in with the stipulation that none of us was ever to walk on her property again. That female dressed me down like nobody had ever done before, even in the military. The man never made an appearance, some said he was dying of cancer. I'll bet he was trying to hurry the end.

We got our cement to the site, made our piers, laid out the foundation and started to form the framework for the floor. Low and behold, Don had made a mistake. We were short six floor joists.

The Airplane

If you are an Alaskan, you have to have an airplane or a boat. I already had a boat so the homestead was a real reason (excuse) for an airplane. I started going through the classified ads and responded to one advertising a PA 11 Piper. This was the forerunner of the Piper Super Cub. This little jewel came equipped with floats, balloon tires and skis. What more could a man ask for? It turned out that it was owned by a partnership, one of which was a guy that I had worked with at Anchorage Sand and Gravel. The price was right so I had it checked out by a licensed mechanic and bought the plane.

This way I could commute from the homestead to Anchorage in all kinds of weather. Because it had floats it opened up a big area around Anchorage with an abundance of lakes in that section of Alaska. Also I could, when on skis, vent my frustrations by practicing, limited aerobatics such as loops, lazy eights, chandelles, stalls, spins etc. It was not stressed for more violent maneuvers. Flying was another enjoyable part of the homesteading experience.

With the lake out, no ice over the swamp, no trespassing on our neighbor's property we were in a pickle. Ah, but old, farsighted Don had bought the airplane. It was on floats, which was good. The only trouble was that, in my training they had taught me Aeronautics, part of that teaching covered the flat plate area of an airplane. Simplified it means that the total square inch area of an aircraft, such as mine, would compare to pushing a board of no more than one square foot through the air. Any major addition to this area by hanging building materials on the outside of the aircraft would alter the flight characteristics to a point where it could be a passport to the next world. I was extremely reluctant to tempt fate, feeling that I had used up all my luck flying combat gliders for Uncle Sam.

One of my best friends was a pilot named Hank. When I told him about my problem he said, "I'll do it." And he did. He just lashed those two by twelves onto the floats and brought them in. Nice guy.

The Cabin

We had bulldozed off the site for the cabin, but had to wait until May for the ground to thaw so we could put in the piers. We used five-gallon paint cans and mixed the site gravel with the cement we had brought in. We laid the beams, the joists and then the 3/4 plywood decking. This, then, was a good work platform for our other carpentry. The A-Frame structure was made of 2x8x20 foot fir which were raised, then covered with 5/8 plywood with the bottom six inched lapping the lower one like a shingle. It was a simple structure, but because it was a weekend project for Dale, his high school buddies, Bob and me, the progress was very slow. We had to drive sixty miles, hike in over the rough country for two miles, then work ten hours or more, hike out and drive home.

Visqueen (polyurethane) sheeting was draped over the windowless openings, which kept most of the rain out, but not the mosquitoes, white sox and no-seeums. You are familiar with mosquitoes. A white sox is a gnat that takes a chunk out of your hide then, I guess, sits on a limb and chaws away. Their bite is painful and slow to heal. The no-seeums are tiny little carnivores that like to get under a sweaty hatband and chew up your forehead. They are small enough to go through a head net so are a real nuisance. I have seen people bitten on the face by no-seeums and they would swell so they could not see out of their eyes.

Because our deadline to move onto the homestead was July 1, our home was a half-constructed, visqueen covered, windowless shelter on that date. Ignorance isn't always bliss. Sometimes it's the first step into a quagmire of work and worry. The more you struggle the faster you sink in. My crew was a great, cheerful, hard working team of teenagers. I hope they carried on some know how from their experience.

In addition to building and clearing we had to find a route to civilization. One day, while the lake was still frozen, an airplane landed on the ice. The pilot introduced himself. "You know Mr. Conover, I've been observing this parcel for several months and would have filed on it, but could never figure a way to build a road out to Big Lake! There does not appear to be access to it!" I didn't even respond. A response requires a reasonable answer. I had none, had never thought that far ahead. Shook me up it did. I was glad when he left.

Back in town I learned that each section line was dedicated as a right of way for access to property. To build a road, we had to find the section line, which was the northern boundary of our quarter section. It had been surveyed in 1914, but we had never been able to find any hubs. Course we had no time to look either!

On the Bureau of Land Management chart it showed a road, Hollywood West, running on that same section line but stopping a mile short of our property. Being ingenious and short of money I devised a scheme to locate the section line through our property. I bought some bunting, tore it into strips about two inches wide and fifteen feet long. I then tied one end around a fist-sized rock, put the streamer in a paper bag. I made up six or eight of these missiles then called my buddy Bob Green. Bob had an Aeronca Champ airplane so we loaded up my bags and took off. Heading west at an altitude of two hundred feet he followed Hollywood West long enough to establish a compass heading that would keep us over the section line over virgin territory. I then, at proper intervals, chucked my markers out the door. They opened and streamed beautifully to the ground.

Back on the ground the family soon found all the markers. We then blazed the trees between them so had a reasonable line to follow to cross our property. Beyond that we used a compass and blazed a path to follow for our road to civilization.

The deadline for moving into the homestead was July 4, 1960. In June we were a long way from being ready. Bobbie had to have major surgery before we moved on the homestead. She was still recovering from that and I was still working in Anchorage as a Sales Manager. I would fly up on weekdays after work and, of course, on Sunday and do what work I could. We weren't getting far with the construction or with the access road.

Another complication was the house in Anchorage. Being a World War II veteran, I could "prove up" on the homestead in seven months by building a cabin, clearing twenty acres and, of course, living there the whole time. One of my friends from another construction company told me he would be delighted to take over our house for the seven months and would house sit, so we assumed that everything was all set. He was going to move in early in July. Four days before we were to leave he told me he wasn't going to do what he had promised.

We placed an ad in the paper but we had no time to pick and choose who was going to stay in our house. We were loading the rental truck, with all the belongings we were going to need at the homestead, when Bobbie finalized the lease with three bachelors. They turned out to be first class tenants. The only problem with the lease was that it gave them tenancy for one year. We had no place to return to at the end of seven months. We opted for a program that allowed us to stay on the property for fourteen months and clear only ten acres.

To get our belongings to the homestead, we rented a truck from one of the local car rental outfits. The manager turned out to be considerably less than honorable. Once loaded we took the lease papers, gathered up Pattie, Russell and Bob, then followed Dale, Mike Rogers, and Ron Cole in the truck in our little Chevrolet sedan. After about an hour and a half we arrived at the Big Lake refuse pile (the dump). This being the nearest takeoff point for our odyssey. We had obtained permission from a Mr. Notti to traverse his land. His homestead was north of the "Tiger Lady" who had banned us forever from her property. I had mentioned to Leonard Gilbert that the "Tiger Lady" stymied us. Leonard told me that Mr. Fred Notti owned the land north of the section line at Big Lake. "Hell, he'll give you permission. Great guy!" He told me where I could write to Fred. I did and got an immediate response. "Go anywhere you want on my property, no problem!" What a wonderful neighbor.

Dale left us to walk into the cabin and bring the tractor and sled out to our embarkation point. I say embarkation because we not only had a dump, but also a swamp to contend with.

A very attractive fourteen-year-old girl appeared and told us that her parents would like for us to come over and have some coffee with them, and get acquainted. We followed to their Quonset type homestead cabin and met Leonard and Francis Gilbert, their daughters Nancy, (our guide) and Lynette. The Gilberts were very cordial. We had coffee, cookies and a nice visit. We gave them the impression, I guess, how simple we thought it was going to be to homestead, what we were going to do, and how fast we were going to do it. We would have everything wrapped up in short order and would soon be living, comfortably, back there. Nancy later told us that when we left they went into hysterics. They even rolled on the floor, laughing at these naive, greenhorn homesteaders.

Dale arrived at the dump site considerable shaken up. He had been knocked off the tractor by a low hanging branch and lay there stunned for awhile. By a God sent miracle he was not killed by the huge sled he was towing. When he came to, he got up, chased the tractor and stopped it.

While the family loaded the sled, I took the bulldozer and made a causeway across the swamp, then cut a trail up the side of a fifty to seventy-five foot hill. It wasn't too steep, but took quite a bit of work with the dozer to get the bank cut enough so I figured we could pull the sled up to the top. I went back to the beginning point, hooked onto the sled and we took off. It was only about two miles to the cabin, so we believed that we could make two trips that day. WE WERE WRONG. It took 26 hours just to get in with the first load.

We had chosen a rainy day. It was drizzling, followed by a driving rain. We made it across the causeway, up the embankment, and about three-quarters of a mile, when one of the sled runners got hung up on a snag and rolled out from under the sled. By now it was coming on evening so I told Bobbie to take Pattie and Russ and walk on in following the cat trail. They left.

Bobbie, "I had never been into the cabin from this side. The cat trail was not any kind of road. We had to go around all the knocked down trees because they were pointing right at us, but it was something to follow. I tried to get the youngsters interested in the area, pointing out the different kinds of trees. There was birch, spruce, aspen and, of course, alder. Hudson Bay tea was a foot-tangling bush that just seemed to be everywhere in the way. Some places Dale had dropped the blade so had uncovered melon sized boulders, upended trees and made it hard for the kids and I to walk. Millions of mosquitoes brought endless torment with their incessant buzzing and biting. Our head nets only allowed a few to enter but that was far too many. The nets also caused a feeling of stuffiness, with the wet net preventing the free passage of fresh air. The children became very tired so kept asking, 'How much further? Where is the cabin?' I had no idea! I started them singing and told them to just put one foot in front of another and we would get there. We finally arrived after walking the last thirty minutes in silence."

"So this, unfinished building is our new home? Only three cots, where will we sleep?"

"I'm thirsty Mom!"

"I'm hungry!"

Don had told me about the stove. An inverted five-gallon

paint bucket with another, right side up sitting on it with a grate on top. "That's my stove? I'm supposed to cook for six or more people with that? LORDY! LORDY!"

Pattie and Russ were all excited, running down to the lake, exploring around the cabin, then coming in and flopping on the cots under the mosquito nets. "OH yes, even in here, there were zillions of the little pests!"

Back at the sled, we unloaded everything, tried to cover it with the plastic, and then assessed the damage. The runner was rolled out, twisting, had ripped the decking so that we could not get it back to any semblance of its original shape. Finally, after an hour or so I said. "We're just going to have to build another sled. Only thing we can do. This thing is hopeless!"

"How about some chow?"

"Yep, that too."

We took off for the cabin.

When we came in, Bobbie had the Coleman lantern going. I said, "What do you think?"

"At least it's different!" She was trying to heat some beans on the stove. The ingenious device I had created wasn't burning very good. I could see that it wasn't getting enough air. I took the top can outside, dumped the fire on the ground, punched some holes in it, near the bottom, put the fire back in it, then took it back into Bobbie. She put the beans back on, then turned to me with tears in her eyes and said, "How do you propose to get rid of this damn smoke?"

After eating some wieners, beans and bread, I and the boys grabbed axes, saws and searched out a couple of trees for sled runners. Because it was July we had twenty hours of daylight so that was a help. After several hours of work we had another sled. So far we had destroyed two sleds on this sojourn called home-steading. We hitched up, went back, loaded all the gear on the new sled and carefully worked our way over deadfalls, skirted sinkholes, twisted through tight stands of alder and eventually arrived at the cabin. A two-hour trip had taken 26 hours. I took one of the cots. My crew also wrapped up in sleeping bags, and we all fell into exhausted sleep for several hours.

Bobbie's description of the cabin:

"I took a break and looked around to see just what I was going to be living and working in for the next 14 months. It was an A-Frame cabin, so we put as much of our supplies back in the space near the floor. Couldn't stand there anyway. The front of the building, facing the lake was covered with visqueen, so we couldn't see out. The north end, which was straight up, was covered with the plastic. It kept most of the rain out, but not the mosquitoes. A sheet of plywood, set on two sawhorses was the table, workspace and pantry. We had paper plates and a bucket of lake water. Who could ask for anything more? We also had no bathroom, not even a privy. Pattie and I took a stroll in the woods, found a suitable, secluded spot with a fallen log at the proper height, and staked out our own private retreat, complete with a can to keep the paper dry."

Our sofa from home was too large to fit into any free space in the cabin so we covered it with plastic and left it outside. Bobbie finally rearranged all the boxes etc. so there was room for this taste of luxury. Dale and I went out to get it. It had absorbed so much rain that when we went to lift it the only parts that came up were the ends. We walked into the cabin, each carrying an end. "Where would you like it placed Ma'am?" After the shock wore off she laughed too, but it was another disappointment for my wonderful wife.

Dale was working at a lumberyard in Anchorage and I was still Sales Manager so we went back to town. This left Bobbie, Bob, Pattie and Russell at the homestead. Bob was fourteen and the man of the house. Patty was eleven and Russell nine. Dale and I both worked six days a week so the only time we had to do anything was on Sunday. I was flying back and forth so accomplished a little in the evenings, but not enough.

Our major need was to get a road out so we could bring in supplies. Bob could run the tractor so worked at that project. He took the bulldozer and worked his way around the trees that were too high, knocked over the ones that weren't and made a passable Jeep trail out to the Gilbert's homestead. He worked on this, intermittently, when he could breakaway from the homestead chores Bobbie assigned to him. His biggest job was to gather wood for the fire, and there were lots of other jobs for him, Pattie and Russ. Bobbie of course was a dynamo of activity, trying to organize and straighten up the house, making things more livable. This was an incredible challenge because the house was so incomplete.

We did all we could to improve conditions that summer. It was also very important to get a supply of wood for the winter. Bobbies uncle, Steve Stevenson, came to visit us and, being a long time logger showed us many of the tricks in falling, bucking and splitting the spruce and birch that would be our winters wood.

Another necessity was a good sled. We had used up three by that time. He showed us how to pick a spruce of about ten inches at the butt, dig out the roots and saw them loose. We then trimmed and cut the tree to the proper length for a runner. Next we trimmed off all the roots but the largest one. The tree had been selected because of it having one large root. This big one was cut so that it formed a curved front runner two feet above the ground. This would allow the sled to rise over humps instead of digging into the ground and thus tearing the runner off the sled, as those had in the past. This sled lasted for years.

Our equipment consisted of a 1952 Chevrolet Sedan, left in town or later at the Gilberts, a 1942 Jeep, old rusty and decrepit, that had cost two hundred dollars and was worth ten times that much to us. Our John Deere 440 tractor cost $4800 dollars. The dealer assured me that it had been through the overhaul shop twice and was in A-One shape. He lied because within a week after we got it into the homestead the hydraulic system on the dozer went haywire. They had to come in and fix that. Then the seat fell off dropping Dale to the ground. If he had been pulling the sled he would have been killed. Our other piece of equipment was a Piper PA-11 airplane. It was yellow and the kids called it Tweety Bird. We had (and used) floats, wheels and skis. It was a two place, 90-horse forerunner of the famous Super Cub.

The jeep road gradually improved, as Bob kept at it. I never realized at that time what a load I was putting on Robert. He was only fourteen, had taken to handling the tractor so easily that I just assumed that he had the know how. Hell, how could he? I knew the danger of "Widow Makers," snags, hung trees, etc. He just learned and survived, no thanks to old Dad. He still speaks to me.

We would take the cat and sled, and later the Jeep, and go out to the Gilberts. There we would transfer to the sedan, then drive into Wasilla or Palmer. We did this for washing clothes, supplies, and groceries, and to go to the doctor. Oh yes, and the vet.

Pluto, Bob's seventy-pound Chesapeake showed up with a face full of porcupine quills. Dale and Mike Rogers, a muscular pair of eighteen-year-olds had all they could do to hold him and pull the quills out. He was then taken to the vet to make sure he had none in his mouth. Didn't cure Pluto, he challenged another spiny fiend later. Not too smart, old Pluto.

I flew back and forth to Anchorage, trying to maintain my job and the homestead at the same time. This proved to be impossible, as we will be shown later.

Another brilliant move on my part was to purchase a second hand chain saw from a neighbor in town. He charged me twenty dollars and sang the praises of this wonderful machine that would take the entire curse out of falling and sawing the wood. I spent more time trying to start the damn thing and keep it running than I would have done just using a bucksaw. Them, at least I understood. Since that time we have had good chain saws, we understand them and can accomplish in minutes what we struggled hours to do then.

Our move had occurred in July of 1960. By fall it was apparent that we would not be ready by the time winter hit us. We didn't have the cabin finished, the wood was not stockpiled in sufficient quantities to carry us even a month. The road needed a lot of work. Things were looking pretty bleak. Bobbie was busy cooking, washing clothes, and trying to make a home. Bob, Patty and Russ all had their chores, carrying water from the lake, gathering wood, picking berries, fishing and of course swimming and playing in the lake and on the beach.

There were moments when we all knocked off and went swimming. I made a primitive raft out of two Styrofoam logs. I put a plywood deck on it, a mast, sail and a rudder. We would tool around on it. It would carry the three kids or Bobbie and I. You couldn't tack with it so was at the mercy of the wind. So who cared? Bob and Dale, while alone one time at the lake, fashioned a canoe type craft. They took two 1x12 boards 12 feet long, put one on top of the other, nailed both ends securely, put a two foot stick in the middle to spread the center. They then wrapped the thing with visqueen climbed in and went fishing. Caught a beautiful 12-inch Kokanee salmon. We had seen fish jumping, but that was the first we had caught.

Later we brought a Boys Life canoe that Dale and his buddy Dave had built when they were about 12 years old. It was made out of squares of 1/4-inch plywood with 1x2 spruce lumber and covered with canvas. They had painted it to make it waterproof. It was joy to use. Even Bobbie and I could glide around the lake after the kids were down for the night. There is no better, more satisfying mode of transporting the body from here to there than a canoe. This canoe was the magical carpet for our entry into the world of the beaver.

The beavers were a constant source of entertainment and wonder. There was a beaver lodge just down the bank from the cabin and two hundred feet from the end of the beach. In the summer we could, at times, see them working on the lodge, adding sticks and mud. In the fall they would start their winter food pile of branches and cut saplings in front of their lodge. The saplings were anchored in place by forcing one end into the muddy lake bottom. The pile would eventually rise above the lake about three feet. They needed an ample supply because when the lake is frozen over they must return to the lodge to get above the water where they can breath, eat and do other necessary life functions. This is their life for up to seven months. There is no access to the lodge except underwater.

Our lake is actually a beaver dam. In a canoe we could work our way through small channels to the dam. It was about one hundred and fifty feet long, stood above the water by about one foot and was made entirely of branches, beaver cut saplings, and mud. An enormous undertaking that had been completed, probably a hundred years before. We know that it was there in 1914 because it was shown on the surveyor's map of that date. The dam requires constant care to keep the leaks repaired and the proper flow of water out of the lake to maintain the desired level. In my experience of building roads in Alaska I have seen dams that we had to dynamite in the road building process, which were repaired overnight by the eager beavers. They are a fascinating wonder of Nature.

Late one evening Bobbie and I were in the canoe and paddled nearly across the lake. We sat with our paddles across our knees, motionless, watching a beaver on the bank. The wind gradually drifted us toward him. Soon we could hear a sound like someone eating celery. Coming closer we learned that he had a Lily pad stem and was sitting there munching away. He quit eating, still unaware of our presence, grasped the stem in his hind feet and slipped into the water, towing the stem. He was coming directly toward the boat and was within fifteen feet when suddenly, we could see, in his eyes, alarm and fright. Slap went his tail and he and the lily pad disappeared in a ring of waves.

Beaver Dam

The engineering skill and the ability of the beaver to construct and maintain their dams had long fascinated me. They were constantly encountered on the streams and creeks of southeastern Alaska. I have sat for hours watching them work when we were constructing the road from Lucky Shot Mine to Willow.

One time Bobbie and I were returning from Fairbanks on the Richardson Highway. When we were approaching Summit Lake I pointed out a valley where Dean, Dad and I had had a fruitless Moose hunt. The hunt turned into a prospecting trip when we found a quartz outcropping with, what we thought was a rich vein of mineralization, gold and all that stuff. We had carried out a hundred pounds of samples, fording the creek numerous times, etc. The samples proved worthless so we had failed in that too. As Bobbie and I got to the south side of the valley we saw that a road had been built, going in to the area I had described. We turned in and soon saw a beaver dam. There was practically no water in the dam. The lodge, sitting out in the middle was high and dry. We could see beaver busily applying mud to the inside face of the dam.

We stopped and watched them for a while. I said, "I thought beaver were supposed to be so damn smart. Here it is late September and the stream will be frozen before they get their dam filled!" I started the car, we broke over a little knoll and "lo and behold" there they were. Two reserve dams holding more than enough water to fill the large dam they were repairing.

The canoe made it possible to explore the beaver dam that had created our lake. The lower end of the lake was an area of ponds and narrow channels. The canoe was the right craft to work your way through the reeds, grasses and brush to the incredible structure the beavers had created, probably at the turn of the century or earlier. We know that the U.S. Bureau of Land had surveyed the area in 1914, nearly fifty years before our time.

The dam itself was four or five feet deep and over a hundred fifty feet long. The outlet drained into a swamp where the channel soon disappeared in the reeds, grasses and brush. This explains the occurrence of the Kokanee (land locked Red Salmon) in our lake. Ours grew to about twelve or thirteen inches in length. Just the right size. They were easy to catch on salmon eggs or with just a piece of red cloth. Russell at ten years could easily keep us in fish. It was fun to watch him because they fight almost as well as a rainbow trout. A great feature of the Kokanee is that, when properly cooked, the skeleton lifts out, tail first, clean as a whistle. No hassle with the bones such as with trout or pike.

The only other fish in the lake was the stickleback minnow, which could sting and infect your hand if you were not aware of the spine in the middle of his back. Fresh water mussels were available. Near our dock was an ever-growing pile of mussel shells left there by the muskrats. These little devils are very secretive. Seldom seen. Must do their deeds at night. In the winter, with the aid of a flashlight, we could see hundreds of tiny fresh water shrimp in the bottom of our water hole, in the ice. We did little ice fishing because of the effort required to chop through the ice three or more feet.

It was a magical experience working the canoe down to the outlet, imagining what it was like when the dam was being created. How they gnawed the trees and branches into lengths, pushed them into position then plastered them with mud with only their tiny front feet to work with. We marveled at the incredible fact that the dam was arched so that the pressure from the water compressed and strengthened the dam, just like the Hoover Dam and others—what a tremendous undertaking for the little guys. I also wondered if the otters that appeared, rarely, on our lake followed the channel up from Fish creek and Cook Inlet.

Loons

The loons, which nested every year on the far side of the lake, were the source of much enjoyment for all of us. Their nest was easily visible from our canoe. We enjoyed a periodic check on the eggs, after sometimes seeing the courting ritual. During this they would rise from the water, flapping their wings and squawking, turning and circling, then subsiding back to the surface. It was a thrill we were lucky enough to witness several times over the years.

The loon with its checkered chest and neck, stately stylish carriage was not blessed with STOL (Short takeoff and landing) capabilities. They struggled mightily, flapping and running along the surface of the water to get airborne, then circling the lake several times to get enough altitude to clear the trees. Landings were fast and splashy.

Only one pair of loons would be on a lake the size of ours. I guess it was a law of nature depending on the food available. Probably the same pair returned every year. They recognized the sound of my airplane engine and would start the alarm several minutes before my plane would become visible to Bobbie and the children. It would call. They would say, "Here comes Daddy!" Sure enough I would become an approaching silhouette soon thereafter.

The loons would shepherd the young or have them on their backs, swimming and calling—what a grand sight to behold. The lonely call of the loon will linger long in our lives. I have experienced no sound that compares with the lonely, soul clutching, call of our Loons. Strangely, the loons who nested on Whale Lake, in our northeast corner, were an entirely different bird with a short, shrill squawk before it dived, not the melancholy call of the Conover loons.

Arctic Tern

The Arctic Tern nested in the swamp spruce near the edge of our lake. The nest would be at the top of a ten or twelve foot tree. There would be up to a dozen nests along the edge and if you approached, too close, would be dive bombed. They are a small white and black bird with a wingspread of, maybe, eighteen inches. The wings are bent forward then back at the leading edge. A tern can hover, flapping mightily, then dive like a rock into the water when a fish is spotted. Unlike the loon it can rise off the water, literally leaping into the air even with a small fish in its beak.

They are very protective of their nest and will dive bomb you if you approach too close in your boat. They screech and drop like a bomb, coming within inches of your head then lofting for another run. If there are several coming from different directions it can be an unnerving experience.

The tern is migratory and can travel from the Arctic coast to the tip of South America (Tierra Del Fuego) which is about eleven thousand miles. Bobbie, Bob, Pattie and Rus traced their probable route on a National Geographic Map, amid speculation of the length of time it would take for the migration. The big question was what inner control started them on the journey and how they navigated that distance in all kinds of weather. The astounding thing, we learned, was that the Tern leaves the nest a scant six weeks after hatching.

Sandhill Cranes

These birds did not return every year, but sometimes spent the summer in the swamp to the east of our lake. We could hear them, but seldom saw them. Never did see any of their young. They are a large, long legged, long necked bird, probably standing five feet high. They, too, have difficulty getting airborne and have a loud, flat call. They migrate in flocks.

One time I was driving along a farm road and there were, probably fifty Sandhill cranes in the field. I had my 8-millimeter movie camera so decided to get a shot. I climbed through the fence, taking pictures, advancing at the same time. Soon I found myself mingling with the flock. They were not bothered at all by my presence.

Elated I continued, gloating at my good fortune, and finally ran out of film. When I went to put in a new roll I found that the one in the camera was a hopeless, tangled mess. Broke my heart it did.

One day while working on the cabin, we saw two people coming across the lake, swimming on air mattresses. It turned out to be Pete and Zona Dahlmann. We used a cruiser for water skiing, for fishing and just putzing around the lake. The cruiser also gave us access to the homestead from another way.

The Dahlmanns occupied the south end of the lake. They had homesteaded a year or so before. They were now building a log cabin, but had taken time off to get acquainted with us and see what we were up to. They turned out to be two of the nicest people in the world, just wonderful neighbors. There was road access to their property that was good enough for our car, so with the cruiser we could come in their way, transfer to the boat and come over to our beach. It was much easier and shorter than our route. The Dahlmanns turned out to be some of the best friends we have ever had. They loved to "borrow" Patty and Russ and treat them royally. We also would picnic together, either at their fire pit or ours.

By the latter part of September we knew that if we were going to prove up on the homestead I would have to quit my job in town. I had to finish the cabin as much as possible and give Bobbie and the children support through the winter. There was no way they could handle the things that must be done without a man around. I reluctantly quit my excellent job, and in October went home to stay.

When I arrived at the Gilberts to become a full time home-steader, Bobbie and the kids were there to meet me with the dozer, sled and, of course, the dogs. When we had transferred everything to the sled Bob took off in fourth gear with the cat and sled. That's over four miles an hour so requires real hustle to your walk to keep up. I did OK for a short while then the soft life of the salesman took over and I began to fade fast. Bobbie though was lean as a greyhound and could walk and talk and easily keep up with the sled. No problem. I finally had to give in and stop long enough to grab a few gallons of oxygen. I made it to the cabin without the indignity of a sled ride. From then on the new regime was in force. I too began to renew unused muscles and tone up the old body.

By this time the airplane was on skis. The freeze-up of the lake is a wonderful experience. We could actually hear the ice cracking when it formed and fully covered the lake. On the first freeze-up we wound up with ice about three inches thick. We could walk on it and as it was almost transparent. We could, at times, see beaver swimming under our feet. They would stop at air pockets to replenish their air supply and then swim on. As the ice grew in depth (we knew how much it was increasing because Bob would report each time he chopped through for water) and still remained slick and smooth. We all got out the ice skates and sleds and had a great time. We would build a fire on the beach and stay and play for hours.

You Holler - We Haul'er - Water That is!

One of the main problems was hauling water. We got it from the lake and had to go through the ice to reach it. Bob's job was to keep us supplied with water. He had to chop through the ice, up to three or more feet in the dead of winter. This meant chopping with an ax, a trench, a foot and a half wide, five or six feet long and deep enough to reach water. He could carry a bucket, and Pattie and Russ could carry another. On Saturday, bath day, it would take all of us to get the water, heat it and perform our ablutions. Took all day. Water supply was a big job for a fourteen-year-old guy.

Hank and Katie Orth gave us a galvanized bathtub. It was about four feet long, butt wide and about fifteen inches high. Sure beat the hell out of a regular round galvanized tub, you could actually sit in it. We would heat the water then two baths later dump it and refill for the next in turn. That made for three cycles for the six of us to get sparkling. I'm sure that Bobbie will have much to offer both on the washing and the bathing

As the days grew shorter and colder we went to bed earlier and arose later. The main struggle was just surviving from day to day, doing what had to be done. We had the once a week trip to town for supplies, snow to shovel, and we had to keep the snow off the airplane, so the wings didn't get overloaded. We had to fight to start the equipment, whether jeep, cat or airplane. It was a time consuming ordeal just to get an engine started and get some work done before dark.

Freezing in the Dark Builds Character

When winter came in late October we were still living in an uncompleted cabin. We were having difficulty getting enough wood. We were in cramped quarters with six of us and two big dogs. The dogs spent most of the time outside but came in at night.

The loft, by this time, furnished with an indoor ladder was the kids' dorm. Up there it was extremely hot when we had the stoves going, while around our feet and lower legs it was cold in the downstairs areas. We used Coleman gas lamps for light, as we had no electricity. The corners of the A-Frame building had no air circulation so got extremely cold when the weather got 10 or 15 degrees below zero. Every morning the water bucket, by old smoky would have up to a half inch of ice on the water. Bobbie and I slept in one corner of the downstairs and it was very cold. The only thing that made it tolerable was the Woods Eiderdown sleeping bag that we opened and covered us.

We had a gasoline powered Maytag washing machine, but it didn't prove practical. Except for the clothes that Bobbie washed by hand, all the washing was done in Wasilla or Palmer. Once a week, if we could get the machinery to run, we would load up the cat and sled or the jeep, go out to Gilberts, and get the Chevy going (if we could). Then we would head for the big city, the washeteria, the grocery store, doing the errands, and then reverse the procedure to get back to the cabin. It was a cold dawn to dark venture.

My lovely sister Reta, wrote from Sacramento, California, where she and her husband Bliss Harper had a big truck repair and army surplus business, and offered to send us a good generator if we would pay the freight. We of course were delighted with the possibility of having electric light to study and read by, so we immediately accepted. A month or so later we received freight billing on an 1800-pound generator, a one hundred and fifty dollar freight bill. I was stunned.

I borrowed my brother Dean's jeep trailer and went down to pick up the generator. It was a monstrous beauty. Six feet long, four feet high and two feet wide. It was big enough to supply power to a small community. I towed it up to Gilberts, hooked the John Deere tractor to the trailer and hauled it into the cabin. I strung lights everywhere, even in the biffy. When we started the thing up the homestead blazed like Las Vegas. We could read and write and draw in any part of the cabin. We used nothing but 200-watt bulbs so it was very revealing, you might say.

Trouble was the sucker burned five gallons an hour so we couldn't afford to run it more than an hour a night. We'd use the gas lamps 'til after dinner and the dishes were done then everyone would get ready. Bob or I would go start the generator and we would read, write, study or whatever until you would hear the monster wind down and die. Total darkness enveloped us as it expired.

Our tractor threw a track. It came off the rollers and front idler. It is a strenuous job to loosen the track tension and then get everything back in harmony and tightened up. In doing all this I re-injured my lower back. There was no way I could stand the trip to town and a doctor so I laid around for a week or so in misery. Then I started to feel a little better so went out to watch the kids slide down the hill and out onto the ice on their sleds. They kept urging me to try it. "Com'on Dad. It's fun! You have to try it!" Finally I settled onto the little sled and took off down the hill. Because I was so much heavier I went twice as fast. At the bottom I flew off the bank and slammed down on the ice. Popped my back in it did! Had no more trouble from then on.

Darkness

The biggest problem, mentally, was the darkness. Being Alaskans we had adapted to the short days and depressing darkness of the long winters while in town. Here it was different. No electric lights except the brief run of the generator. No television, movies, plays, school functions—all the little diversions that accompany town living. Now the cold and the inability to do the simple chores without a lantern or flashlight complicated any outside chores.

A gasoline lantern is bright and glares so that a direct look at it is almost painful. They are noisy, and the mantle so delicate that a slight bump on the base will cause it to disintegrate. When this happens you must go through the drill of installing a new one. First you turn off the gas valve, let it cool, and then remove the damaged mantle. Now the new one, a mesh type cloth bag, is tied onto the jet with an asbestos string, then fluffed 'til it is as round as you can get it. You then light it with a match and let it burn to an ash. Now you have a workable mantel but I repeat it is made out of ash so must be handled as gently as a newborn baby. If you are careful enough the mantel will last for weeks. The lantern is far better than a candle but does not compare to electric lights. The lantern can be dangerous if it should develop a leak. It could catch fire and destroy you house in minutes in the bush. You learn to be alert.

The interminable darkness can be the major cause of "Cabin Fever" which afflicts all Alaskans in the winter to some degree. It and the constant cold have destroyed marriages, partnerships and the peace of mind of even the most rugged folk.

Free Land

The lure was free land. The reality was endlessly frustrating turns, twists and changing tactics to turn things around to continue on the chosen path—SURVIVAL.

"The saw won't start; the water bucket's frozen; the tractor threw a track; the dogs got a face full of Porcupine quills; need more firewood; the stove won't bake; we need to wash clothes; it's 53 degrees below zero; road needs plowing; low on lantern gas; haven't seen the sun for ten days; Christmas is coming, no presents; need canned milk and groceries; also batteries for the radio."

Heard on the radio about the homesteader, near Wasilla, who got so fed up he set fire to his house, barn, and truck—everything that would burn. Just sat back and watched it go. We roared with laughter. Knew just how he felt. Could have done it a dozen times.

"Mr. James is being held pending psychiatric evaluation."

"Felt like going over to testify that the guy just had enough. Wanted to be free of the hassle. Give him a ticket to the States and your blessing."

As the days grew shorter and colder we went to bed earlier and arose later. The main struggle was just surviving from day to day, doing what had to be done. We had the once a week trip to town for supplies. We had snow to shovel. We had to keep the snow off the airplane, so that the wings didn't get overloaded. We had to fight to start equipment, whether jeep, cat or airplane. It was a time consuming ordeal just to get an engine started and get some work done before dark. In the dead of winter daylight could be three hours or less.

I got a blowtorch heater with the airplane. I had a flexible metal exhaust pipe that was about ten feet long and 3 inches in diameter. I had a canvas cover that I would place over the engine of the plane. It extended down to the ground. I would place the end of the flexible pipe under the engine with the other end connected to the blowtorch. It was a matter then of cranking the blowtorch to feed air to the flame and to send the hot air through the pipe to heat the engine of the plane. The kids and I would take turns on the crank until the engine was warm. Then it was necessary for Bob to pull the propeller through to start the engine—a scary chore for a 14-year old boy standing on an icy lake. He had to grasp the propeller blade, swing his right leg straight and high, throw his leg down and back while pulling on the propeller. His leg would pull him away from the blade if all went well. This was especially hair raising when the engine started and you were standing a foot or so from a whirling, lethal five-foot propeller blade.

Immediately on landing, after a flight, I would drain the oil from the engine, while it was still hot, put it in a can and take it to the cabin to sit behind the stove. When I wanted to fly I had hot oil to pour into the engine. Sort of an operation HEAD START.

Starting the cat or jeep was a similar ordeal involving the blowtorch. One time we were trying to go to Palmer to buy Christmas supplies. We cranked all day on the blowtorch, trying to get the jeep started. Never did make it. Found out that the temperature was 55 degrees below zero. That temperature held on for several days then rose to 20 below. It was like a heat wave. We were running around with no coats or sweaters on.

Bobbie's Poem
"The Trusty 42 or Jessie"

They got up bright and early before the sun had riz.
They were going to the city to take care of Christmas biz.

The kids came down the ladder just as happy as could be
With cheeks as red as ornaments a hanging on the tree.

Ma was busy at the stove with flapjacks big and round.
Pa was loading up the jeep they'd soon be city bound.

He pressed the starter button so she could warm a bit
Before she started on that long, cold fifty-mile trip.

He held the button down awhile but she wouldn't even fire.
The only thing that functioned was poor old pappy's ire.

The sun was creepin' o'er the hill the battery ran low.
He called her a few choice names but still she wouldn't go.

He checked the wiring and the gas; he checked the spark
plugs,too.
Said he'd try her just once more but nothing would she do.

He got another battery and jumped her then and there.
The sun was then 'bout halfway up but she didn't seem to care.

So then he got the ether can and squirted at the carb,
And said "By Gad! We'll get there yet! So don't give up," to Barb.

Well the sun went down, still he worked to make that old jeep go,
But she was stubborn as a mule and wouldn't even show.

He came back into the house chilled clear to the bone,
And said, "I guess we just can't go." The kids began to moan.

He'd try her in the morning and if she wouldn't go
He'd start the old Bulldozer and drag her through the snow.

"Then by Gad she'd go!"

Our Christmas tree was decorated almost entirely with ornaments that Bobbie and the kids made from whatever was handy.
We had strings of colored popcorn, and dozens of figures and
shapes that were crafted with imagination and ingenuity. We had
a beautiful tree and a memorable Christmas.

My sister, Reta, sent us some apples and nuts. Bobbie put
them in the Christmas stockings. The apples froze solid by
morning. It was dark; it was cold. We huddled around the little
tin stove. We would fill it with spruce firewood and it would get
cherry red and just dance. You had to keep turning you body, like
you were on a spit, to heat your parts evenly. You would finally
give up and get dressed. Lots of wool. Socks, underwear, shirts,
pants, sweaters, and of course, knitted wool hats.

Dale had taken off work from the lumberyard in Anchorage
to come up for Christmas. Because of the extreme cold (fifty-
five below zero) it was a week before we could get out, get his
car started and see him off to Anchorage.

Pluto, our big Chesapeake dog was freezing in the cold
weather. He would get so close to the stove that he would singe
his hair. We later found out that what he needed was fat so on

one of my trips to Anchorage in the plane, I stopped by Jack's Food Market and picked up some suet. We put that in Pluto's food and in a matter of days he was fatter, his fur glistened and he no longer shivered. Guess the body needs fat in a cold climate.

Another thing I remember about that cold spell was the sound of the ice cracking. You would hear it in the middle of the night; a roar would startle you awake. The next morning you would see a crack in the four-foot ice extending clear across the lake.

We used to stand outside in the night and watch the stars. Bobbie and the three children had studied the heavens so could point out the constellations. It was a magic time because of the dark sky, the brilliant stars hanging just right there. On the horizon we could see the orange glow of Anchorage, twenty air miles away, sixty some by road.

Northern Lights

One of the big bonuses we enjoyed was to go out on the lake on a cold, dark winter night and witness the electrifying, elec-tro-magnetic experience of the Aurora Borealis. We watched the Northern Lights.

The family would group, maybe fifty yards out on the ice. There the whole canopy of the sky was a black backdrop, sprin-kled with diamonds, for shifting curtains of color that danced from one horizon to the other. The entire heavens were alive. Delicate, iridescent greens, blues, reds and mixes of these hues, in crinkled bands, never constant, would flare, fade, and then van-ish. New bursts would blossom in random spots evoking gasps of "OH! Look over here." "Did you see that?"

With no artificial light to hinder the extravaganza we could watch until sated with rapture, or until the Gods wrote finis to the visual symphony of the skies. At times we could hear crackling as the kaleidoscope scene shifted its position to a new setting on the horizon. It seemed that we and the stars were the only witnesses to the shimmering sheets of subdued shades, the rainbow hues magically moving from one celestial segment to another, flaring brightly, holding briefly, then fading after only a moment of life.

In extreme cold your ax will rebound from a tree like it was rubber. Makes it dangerous doings. Also if you fell one tree into another, the second tree will sometimes shatter and you have a shredded trunk. When the cold snap ended it was such a relief to enjoy the twenty-five below heat spell. We could peel off a cou-ple of layers of clothes, get the machinery running and actually accomplish some work.

Teaching School

Because it was impossible to get Bob, Pattie and Russ out to Big Lake every day of the week to school, Bobbie arranged with the State to get a Calvert Correspondence Course for the children. That, of course, instantly added "Teacher" to her many chores.

The manuals came and each child had their assigned lessons. It was very thorough and required diligent effort to complete each assignment. Each day's assignment had to be completed before moving on to the next. The course manuals did not arrive until late October so the school period extended to the middle of the following summer. The school period would be interrupted by sunshine, migrating geese, a moose in the lake, otter on the ice, anything novel and interesting. Some daily lessons would take more than a day to complete. All the work was graded in Chicago and the last scores were eagerly awaited. The kids were all ahead of their classmates when they resumed public schooling in Anchorage. Pattie and Russell's Calvert School's records were accepted without question. For some weird reason the High School's administration downgraded Robert's excellent Calvert grades forcing him to repeat his grade—a senseless, devastating blow to him.

Another problem was that the "Town Kids" would not accept our children back in their old relationships. They were looked on as country bumpkins and faced the cold shoulder of the smug classmates. New friendships had to be created which was a hard period of time for Bob, Pattie and Russ. Human Nature!

Mukluk Telegraph

Mukluks are footwear worn by Eskimos and others in the far north. They are made with sealskin bottoms, caribou or reindeer uppers and are a wonderful solution to the problems of the northern world.

Mukluk Telegraph was the nightly radio program from Anchorage that relayed messages to the isolated people of the area, homesteaders, trappers, miners, commercial fishermen, etc. We listened religiously each evening and were thrilled when someone was kind enough to remember us with a message. The announcer read these messages so they came through with all the emotion, humor or other true feelings of the sender. You developed a kinship with people you would, probably, never meet.

Every subject imaginable would eventually find its way to Mukluk Telegraph --- "From Molly, baby will be born tomorrow, --- Jack's mother passed away --- Junior graduated, head of his class at ---We're flying over to pick blueberries, be there at 12, --- Got any moose staked out? --- To Herman at Rolly Joe Lake, I took a shortcut and buried the John Deere. Can you walk your dozer over and pull me out --- Could use a thirty feet of half inch cable if you have it. Ed. ---To Joe at Pee Pee Lake, Marge says to shove it! She isn't coming back!" Some of the problems had all the elements of a continuing soap opera and were followed as avidly as those on television in town.

Survival Training

Bobbie and I were very conscious of the need to have some survival know how drilled into the children. Pattie and Russell were never to leave the cabin area alone in severe weather. Each carried matches and were taught how to build a fire by using the tiny twigs and moss from the bottom branches of the spruce trees. They acted like tinder and with a supply of increasingly larger twigs and limbs they could have a fire in no time. Pealing birch bark and using that would also work fine, but if the bark was taken all around the trunk (ringed) it would kill the tree. In deep snow you could use your bow (Swede) saw to cut several 30 inch pieces from a 4 or 5 inch green spruce tree, lay them on packed snow and build the fire on that. It could last for hours.

They were also made aware that in the remote possibility of being alone in deep snow in a bad blizzard they were to dig a cave in a drift, crawl in there and stay 'til found or the storm was over. Fortunately we never had a survival crisis, but the knowledge of what to do was reassuring.

Another caution—never touch metal with your bare hand in very cold weather. Your fingers would stick to the metal and if you jerked your hand away the skin stayed. Very painful and a long time healing.

They were cautioned about running when there was a danger of freezing the lungs. Another must was dry socks and mittens. At 50 degrees below zero we used "Bunny Boots" which were Army surplus felt boots. Thick, white felt for the sides and with a heavy insole over the leather sole, they were comfortable in the coldest weather. The trouble was that they were all men sized boots so were a problem for the smaller children. Worked though.

Because the laundry was a once a week chore and a limited wardrobe did not provide fresh socks daily, the nights were scented by damp socks drying on overhead racks. Like many other things we just got used to it.

Time for a Poem.

Biffy

Coming awake she was aware of the cold and a sense of urgency. Opening her eyes she lay for a moment staring into the darkness. Rolling away from the wall she could see, over his shoulder, some light on the ceiling beams. Big and warm, he was also a barrier. Out from under, up and over. Instant ice needles thrust for her bones. She jammed her feet into cut-offs, wrestled into a parka, left the cabin and hurried up the path.

She paused. The quiet was like a soft, thick blanket that enveloped her completely. She could see millions of diamonds glistening in the snow, both on the ground and in the trees. The black sky, with no earthlight to interfere, made the perfect backdrop, as GOD intended, for the brilliant display of his stars. Urged on by the penetrating cold she also felt the need to start a poem.

Biffy

When it's forty below and through ice and snow
THE BIFFY IS FAR AWAY
Then there's nothing sadder than a full, full bladder
You must go. You cannot stay
But by the same token, it must be spoken
And you will hear it said
That there's nothing gladder, than an empty bladder
And a warm, warm, warm, warm bed.

191

Moose

After a day of falling trees and hauling them into camp we were having dinner. "We have to get some meat." Bobbie stated.

"OKAY," I said. "Bob, why don't you get up at daybreak. There will probably be a moose where we fell those birches. They like the birch leaves. Take the rifle and go up there and get a moose!"

"OK. Dad, I'll do that!"

It was barely light when Bob left. A gunshot and soon the sound of running feet awakened me. Bob burst through the door.

"Dad, Dad I got one! He ain't dead yet!"

"Take it easy Bob, I'll just be a minute."

I hurried into shoes, pants and shirt, grabbed a coat and hat and we trotted back up to the site. The moose was down, but struggling. I took the rifle and made a head shot. It died.

"Good job, Bob. Let's go have some breakfast, then we'll come back and dress it out. "

After breakfast Bobbie announced, "No school today. We will all go up there and learn how to take care of a moose!"

As the kill was in the flight pattern of the Big Lake Airstrip, and knowing how squeamish Alaskan pilots are about the sight of blood, we strung a big piece of visqueen over the kill. As it was white, it would blend in with the snow pretty well. Everyone watched as I, with the help of Bob, gutted, skinned, and quartered the animal. We then brought the tractor and sled up to the kill, loaded it on and hung it all in the woodshed. Because we were living in a "deep freeze" we had no trouble keeping the meat. We would just cut off a hunk, cook and eat. The next trip out we gave a hindquarter to the Gilberts.

The Gilberts

The Gilberts, Leonard, Frances, Nancy and Lynette were great neighbors. Leonard, a WWII Vet, had been a tail gunner on B29s in the Orient. He told us about seeing a Turban topped native fishing, several miles out on the Indian Ocean. The Pilot, the hot-rock type, was cruising along at about 20 feet and headed straight for the fisherman. As Leonard passed over the fisherman, spear raised in defense, he tumbled over backwards into the water. Leonard would just roar with laughter when he described it.

The Gilberts had homesteaded several months before us and had their problems. The biggest being over what defines a residence. Leonard and the two girls had moved into a Quonset Hut on their 80 acres. Frances lived in Anchorage as she had a good job with the Corps of Engineers.

After seven months on the land Leonard called for an inspection so he could apply for his Patent for full ownership. When the Bureau of Land Management Team learned that Frances had lived in Anchorage they turned down the application.

"Your residence, Sir! Is where your wife resides, Sir!"

This, of course, meant that the Gilberts had to start all over and with no income. When we met them they were in Phase II and were having a lean, mean time of it. With their fantastic sense of humor they could laugh even while telling the story.

We left our Chevrolet sedan at their place. There was good, maintained road from there to town. On one of the trips we were just leaving Gilbert's field when we looked back and saw Pluto, our big Chesapeake dog running, proudly, with a huge shiny, white bone. We were puzzled as to where he had gotten such a prize. On the next trip out we learned that the Gilberts used an old panel truck for a freezer. With daily temperatures zero or below it worked fine. Someone had left the door of the panel open and Pluto had spent the day, while we were in town, feasting on their last roast. Leonard and Frances went into hysterics telling us about it. Couldn't stop laughing. We felt bad about it so Bobbie picked out a nice big beef roast while in Palmer.

"No Way! No Way! Thank you very much but No Way!" They would not even consider taking the beef. Trouble was we knew they could certainly use it.

We had a hand crank ice cream freezer. Leonard loved the ice cream Bobbie made and would do the grinding when they visited.

Leonard called for his second inspection. He learned from this group that his Quonset hut (residence) was not on his land. He was required to move it a couple of hundred feet, but the BLM did not require him to put in another seven months. Got their Patent they did!

The next time we saw them they had sold the homestead for $8,000 bucks, bought a new car, made two trips to the states and were broke.

Breakup

Breakup is the term used in the north when Mother Nature is struggling to change the land and water from the dark, frigid grasp of the white, white winter, to the greens, blues, browns and yellows of spring. This change is not sudden but is parceled out in bits and pieces—not necessarily small pieces. A willawa wind can rapidly alter the lake or landscape. Snow becomes wet and heavy—ice crackles and creaks. Brown and green bottomed bowls sit under the spruce, aspen and birch trees. The white sides gradually subsiding 'til the forest floor has shed winter. The vibrant growing season has arrived. It starts in April, but will take until the middle of May to mature and bring the period of pencil ice to the lake. The ice always first thaws around the edges, gradually retreating to the center of the lake. The body of ice changes its structure and takes the form of pencil like crystals, with very little cohesion. A very dangerous time to venture on the lake ice. Patches of water appear in the ice mass and then a strong wind will appear, and the ice will grind, growl and disappear.

Bob has always loved sailing, still does. One time when the lake was almost ready to open, he took our pram, and raised the sail. The pram was only 8 feet long and not more than 30 inches wide. The mast was two different diameters of electrical conduit about 10 feet high—far too heavy for this gentle craft.

This time he had about 150 feet from the shore to the ice pack so sailed down the lake, came back and was going to come about. As he let the boom out, a gust hit and the pram flipped. Bob barely got wet, I swear he walked the 150 feet to shore on top of the frigid water—a repeat of Jesus' feat.

Our cabin sat about 40 feet above the lake on a point of land. The bluff going down was pretty steep. We were going to bring our sixteen-foot cabin cruiser boat to the homestead, so would require a road down to the lake. We took the dozer and cleared a way. When we had pushed the overburden away we discovered that the bluff was nearly pure sand. We pushed the sand down to the lake and had a nice sandy beach about 75 feet long and 12 feet deep. This made it a lot more enjoyable when we went swimming.

While the lake is going through the throes of transition, the land, with the snow gone and more heat from the sun, begins to thaw. Cleared land gets a little muddy, deeper mud, then disaster. The disaster only occurs if you try to drive a car, jeep or tractor over an unimproved homestead road before the ground has thawed and the first two feet of mud can drain to a dry state. Where we were the cleared ground could freeze to a depth of 8 feet, so it took some time to be passable.

Later an extended period of rain can make the road a mire.

The Jeep

The Jeep had been bought from Pat Kelly. Pat was a pilot for Reeve Aleutian Airways and had flown this old relic from Shemya, far out on the Aleutian Chain. He had bought it surplus and had flown it back to Anchorage. We were delighted to give him two hundred dollars for it. Best buy I ever made in a motor vehicle. It was beat up, battered and bruised, but we repainted it with a sickly light green paint and put it to work. In the several years we had it we never had a major repair on it.

A lot of people think that a four-wheel drive vehicle will go anywhere. It won't! When they get reckless, as all four-wheel drivers do, it just means that they will be stuck far worse than you could ever be in a conventional two-wheel drive vehicle.

This is a true incident. We were driving to Kenai Lake from Anchorage. The road alongside the Turnagain Arm has many points of land that you have to drive around. On one point we encountered a huge boulder that had rolled down the mountain and was sitting in the middle of the pavement. It was five or six feet high and at least four feet across. It was sitting in a hole in the pavement over a foot deep.

I stopped and sent some of the kids each way to stop the motorists and warn them of the hazard. A citizen in a new Bronco pulled up, got out and surveyed the situation. (This was when the Bronco first came out with four-wheel drive. A brand new feature in the car.) The guy says, "I'll just hook onto it and pull it out of the way! I've got four-wheel drive!"

I was stunned. I was a heavy equipment operator. I knew that it would be a big job for a D7 or D8 Caterpillar tractor to budge the damn thing. I said, " I don't think I would try that!"

He said, "Oh! It's no problem. I've got four-wheel drive."

We stood fascinated while he rustles around in the rig and finally combines tire chains and others, and damned if he doesn't come up with enough to hook onto the boulder.

I said again, "I don't think I would try that."

His wife said, "John, I think you should listen to the man!"

He puffs up, "Honey! I've got four-wheel drive!" He steps into the car, puts it in gear, races the engine and lets out the clutch. The engine screams then shrieks, but the brand new Bronco sits still. The transmission, the rear end or both are busted. De-stroy-ed.

We just got in the car and drove away.

Stuck

It was always preferable to use the jeep for the trip out to the Gilberts and back. That is, of course, if the road was passable. We had gone through a rainy period, followed by a couple of days of sunshine.

"I have to go to town. Do you think the road is okay?"

"Could be. I'll fly over it and see what it looks like. If it's OKAY, I'll wag my wings on the way to town. (I was still working in Anchorage.)

"OKAY, check it out!" I really couldn't see much from a couple of hundred feet. The tree branches obscured a lot of the road, but I decided it looked OK. Going over the cabin I wagged as the whole family looked on and waved.

It was pushing seven o'clock in the evening when I got in the pattern to land that evening. I could see that the jeep was not there so gunned the engine and headed down the road. About a mile and a half away, I spotted the jeep mired in a mudhole, still facing away from the cabin. Bobbie and the kids were working to free it. Must have been there nine hours or more.

I landed at the cabin, changed clothes, grabbed an ax and shovel, and headed for the scene.

My lovely wife didn't even look up. Seemed to be really angry about something. We jacked up the jeep, got some branches under the wheels and finally got back to the cabin. After the chill thawed she told me. "The kids heard the plane. Here comes Daddy! Here comes Daddy!"

"I told them, DON'T EVEN WAVE!" Bobbie and the children were stuck many, many times, but that was the worst time when they were alone.

The River Kwai

One time the five of us were on our way out in the Jeep and we came to the swamp the kids called The River Kwai. We stopped at the edge and pondered. It seemed to be deeper and the top three inches of the water was ice slush. Should we or shouldn't we chance it. If we got stuck in the middle it would be a wet two-mile hike back to the cabin. Then I said, "What the hell!" and stamped on the throttle.

"It's a lot deeper! Gawd! What have I done? We're going to be sitting out here. What if the fan gets bent and ruins the radiator?"

Ole Jessie just kept on rolling and pushing a hill of ice ahead, water was coming in over the floorboards, the exhaust sounded muffled and gurgley, but we kept moving. Just before we got to the other side the motor coughed. I thought we would get dunked, but old "Jessie" climbed the bank, coughed again and died. I had to get rid of all the ice, and then I raised the hood. The spark plug wells were full of water so had finally shorted the system. I baled them out, and dried the plugs. Good old Jessie got us through. On the return trip the water level was, mysteriously, lower so we cruised on through the Kwai to the cabin.

Tune - Cruising down the River.

Jessie

Cruising down the byway in our trusty forty-two
Where every bump you skin your rump
Each time it's someplace new.
The creek is always muddy. The swamp's a challenge, too,
While we go bumping down the highway in our trusty forty-two.
The chains go clang. The tires go bang.
The wiring melts away.
Roots scrape the pan. They stick in the fan,
Which means another delay.
The six of us together are always black and blue
While we go cruising down the byway in our trusty forty-two.

Mushrooms

Bobbie made a study of Mushrooms. She had an excellent book that had clear photos of the various varieties. There are so many that it's difficult to distinguish from similar appearing ones, which are poisonous or even deadly. We settled on one. The Birch Bolete was easy to recognize, having a brown top with the underside a dirty cream color. The underside had the appearance of a sponge with tiny tubes throughout its surface. If you discarded the spongy part it was excellent in taste and texture. They grow up to six or eight inches in diameter so furnished a substantial amount of food. They could be dried easily so we gathered as many as we could, for future use.

We also gathered blueberries, and low bush cranberries, (the Scandinavian Lingonberry) which are far superior to the cranberries available in the stores for Thanksgiving and Christmas. They are easy to pick with the Swedish berry picker and will keep for a year or more in just plain water. In the olden days the Scandinavians made them part of the diet aboard ship to prevent scurvy. They are very high in vitamin C. It worked and still does. They make an excellent sauce to be served with caribou, moose and, of course, beef. We also made cranberry liquor out of them —really great.

Mossberries grow half hidden in the moss. They are small black berries, no good by themselves, but when the juice is added to crabapples, blueberries etc. as an extender the result is excellent jelly or jam. Currants were also great for jelly, one of our favorites. On rare occasions we picked Salmon berries, but never in quantities sufficient for preserves or pie.

Bobbie also educated us on the poisonous berries, such as the baneberry. On one occasion at another area, I saw her save a family from serious consequences. They had a beer box full of baneberries, thinking they were low bush cranberries. They had enough to poison half of Anchorage.

We never made a study of roots and herbs that the natives utilized and we regret that. We had heard that the root of the Lilly Pad was edible. It looked like an oversized Pineapple, but we never got around to trying that either. We did try tapping the birch trees for their sap with the idea of making syrup (as per Maple Syrup), but it proved to be not a worthwhile effort.

We put in a small garden and raised carrots, potatoes, radishes, lettuce, etc. but it was newly cleared earth and not mature enough as an agricultural soil to be a bountiful truck garden.

Russell's Cabin

Russell decided to build a cabin. He searched out and found spruce trees 3 to 4 inches in diameter. He trimmed, then cut them in seven-foot lengths. He nailed the corners without fitting them so there was a space between the logs. It turned out structurally sound so I brought two 3\8-plywood sheets for his gabled roof.

He had a doorway, but no door. Pete Dahlmann must have measured the opening, cause one day he brought over a slab door with leather hinges. He reinforced the framework, installed the door complete with a sliding latch. A neat, neat neighbor. Russ and Pattie had a great time making chairs, tables, and the necessary fixin's for a house.

Clearing Land

One of the requirements to getting a Patent (own a homestead) was to clear and plant 20 acres. Because we had rented our house for a year, thus would have no home to return to, we chose the option of 14 months residence and the clearing of 10 acres. We also had to pay a penalty of a couple of hundred dollars.

I chose the area north and west of the lake because it would be the easiest to clear. It was the lowest area with trees no more that ten or fifteen feet high. Dale was eighteen and had several muscular buddies volunteered to help—Mike Rodgers, Mike Guthrie, Ron Cole, and Leroy Henderson. So Bob and I, Dale and his buddies went to work. We started when the ground was still frozen. We measured the area to be sure the clearing would be big enough, then went to work. As Dale's crew was still in high school they would come on weekends. Bob, with Bobbie, Pattie, Russell, and I would work on it in the meantime. When we had it all slashed I hired a man with a D7 Dozer to come in and clear it. He piled the trees, brush, moss and some dirt in windrows, leaving bare land that we could plant.

The stipulation was that you had to plant a crop. No mention was made as to harvesting or that it had to be a good, profitable crop—just a crop. We planted Brome Grass. The land was not good farmland so the crop was negligible. We had fulfilled our clearing and planting requirements.

Tweety

Tweety was Pattie's parakeet. We did not bring her up to the homestead until the next summer. As soon as the weather was warm enough, on a trip to town in the airplane I picked her up from my brother's house. She had been there for a year. Tweety had been taught to talk by Pattie and Bobbie, but had added to her vocabulary in the interim.

The change to the homestead setting must have been a remarkable experience for her. Now she could see and hear the birds at the feeder and was constantly excited and talking.

A new phrase that popped up from her was, "Now, you listen to me Jimmy!" It was a perfect imitation of the voice of my sister-in-law, Betty talking to her new son-in-law Jimmy. We could hardly wait to see Betty and rib her about that one.

Tweety survived the homestead experience and lived to a ripe old age back in town. She sometimes had to share her cage with Russell's chameleon and watched in fascination as Pattie's garter snake slithered around on the floor during its free time.

Leeches

"Russell, Come here!"

Russ was sitting in an innertube, floating about 20 feet off shore. When he paddled to Bobbie she grabbed his foot, took a salt shaker from her apron and salted the leeches clinging to his toes. There was a mamma and several baby leeches. The salt caused them to turn to a liquid, which dropped off.

"Don, what can we do about these leeches? They're awful!"

"Dunno! Next time we're in town I'll call the Fish and Wildlife." This I did.

"Hello, how can I help you?"

"Sir, we are homesteaders on a lake. We have a problem with leeches when we swim. The children, especially as they sit on a raft or tube and have their feet dangling in the water. What can we do about that? How can we kill them?"

A long pause.

"Well, the best way is to get two flat rocks. Place the leech on one and then strike it with the other rock. Works every time."

I had no response.

"I'm sorry for that. Seriously, the only way you can get rid of the leeches in your lake is to kill all the fish, leeches, etc. by poisoning the lake with a root called Rotenone. This requires a lot of time and expense. How large is your lake?"

"Well, twenty five or thirty acres."

"Hmm! That would be expensive, you see Mr. Conover the leech is a survivor. They have been around for over 250,000 years. They are also bisexual so do not mate. Each one can do the whole thing. I suggest you just co-exist, bear with them."

"OK, Sir. Thank you!" Close inspection and salt was the watchword. It worked.

As an experiment I took a leech with several babies suckling on it, put them in a jar then filled the jar half full of lake water. When we moved back to town I took the jar along.

It was nearing Christmas, and the leeches had been in the jar since July. They were never fed and the babies never left the Mother/Father--both? None of the creatures seemed to have shrunk from the original size very much. The water was green with algae and had a slight odor. I had added a little water a time or two but that was all.

As Christmas was just a few days away I took on the caring, loving spirit of the season. After my martini one evening, I decided to lend a hand to my captives. I would feed them. Next day would be liver and onions day at the Conover household. All that blood would be great for my friends.

We picked up some calf's liver and that evening I took a small piece, dropped it in the water and stirred it with my finger. Instantly Mama and all the little leeches were trying to get latched to my finger. Forget the liver.

The water turned bloody and I thought, "All's well in the leech world." The sad, sad ending is that next morning Mrs. Leech and all the little suckers were dead.

Bobbie Rae

One of the big, "We're gonna's" that was discussed a lot during the winter was: "Were gonna bring the boat in and water ski!"

Once the lake was out and the road passable I went to town and hooked onto the sixteen foot Chris Kraft Cabin Cruiser we had. It was called a cabin cruiser because the front 8 feet was decked over and had port holes in the sides and a door in front. At Gilberts we changed from the car to the John Deere tractor to pull it. The trip in pretty much destroyed the road in places with the trailer wheels pushing a foot and a half of mud. We finally arrived at the cabin amid cheers, backed down to the lake and launched the "Bobbie Rae."

When we decided to homestead we had joined the Anchorage Health Spa. It was vital that all the kids be able to swim. Dale and Bob could already, but Pattie and Russ learned there. Bobbie had never learned to swim. Her mother had instilled a fear of the water in Bobbie and her two sisters. In spite of her fear, Bobbie had taken the children to Big Lake, to my brother Dean's cabin. I would bring the boat up there and they would swim and water ski for a week at a time. Now we had the boat on our lake. We brought gas in by the drum for the boat and the airplane, which was now on floats. All the kids were excellent water skiers and even old Don made it around the lake on one ski—once.

We would have water ski parties with the Dahlmanns and their friends. Barbecuing ribs or Salmon. What a special time to remember! The real treat, was when Pete would ski. They had a fourteen-foot aluminum skiff, which they powered with a 15 horsepower engine. Incredibly, Zona could pull Pete, who is six foot six with that boat. He would start from the dock, always wore a long, flapping bathrobe and would reach down, take off one ski, put it under his arm and go around the lake on one ski. After a while he would put the ski back on and zoom around, robe straight out behind. Pete and Zona were always in high spirits and great company.

Zona, a schoolteacher by profession, spent hours visiting and teaching Pattie and Russ, and the kids thoroughly enjoyed her company. Pete a naturalized American citizen, from Germany, would bring his parents over from Germany to visit. They would stay at the cabin during the week while Pete and Zona were working. They would come up on the weekends. Mr. Dahlmann, senior, spoke broken English and called Bobbie, Mrs. Pi -o-neer. We enjoyed them very much and also the senior Miles, Zona's parents when they came up from Michigan.

Pete built a large raft, using big Styrofoam logs. It was anchored at their end of the lake, but we were free to use it at any time. We would take our guests down to his raft and catch fifteen or twenty Kokanee salmon in a half-hour or so. The Kokanee would fight almost as good as a Rainbow. They are a good fish to fry—nice taste and the bones lift out all in one piece. Good eating.

The Dock

To build a dock on a lake that freezes to a depth of three or four feet presents a problem. If you choose to build a floating dock it must be pulled ashore for the winter. A permanent dock usually requires that wooden piling be driven which, of course, is not practical on an isolated lake. To prevent the huge, wind driven ice chunks from destroying the dock during spring breakup, I chose to build an island.

We took two fifty gallon diesel drums, cut the top out, sunk them twenty feet off shore and filled them with gravel. Next, an army cot bed frame was placed around them. We then made a four by seven-foot structure out of two by twelve lumber. This was like a topless and bottomless box. We re-enforced the corners with galvanized metal, then placed it so it was surrounding the drums. This was, then, sunk and the whole thing filled with gravel. The box extended above the surface by a foot or so. We then decked that, floated two twenty-four foot logs over, ran them from the bank to the dock, decked them and we were in business. We used this for years, only replacing the logs once.

Transition Time

A wonderful part of the experience was that we were sitting in the middle of 160 acres. That is one/half mile on each side of a square. We asked no one whether or not we could build this, do that, whatever. That freedom grows on you and we spent a lot of time trying to find a way to continue living on the homestead.

The timber was not sufficient for logging, and it wasn't practical to farm. We got excited about dredging the lake bottom and selling it for garden soil. It was no good. Sphagnum moss was plentiful in some areas. I researched the agricultural use of peat moss. I found that most of it, used on the West Coast, came from New Westminster on Vancouver Island in Canada. My information stated that their deposits were near depletion. Not more than a couple years supply remaining.

I flew down there to check the operation. They refused to allow me in the place. I chartered a helicopter and hovered over their operation long enough to get pictures of the process.

Back in Alaska I determined that there were large deposits of Sphagnum near the Nikiski natural gas deposits on the Kenai Peninsula. Natural gas is necessary for the drying process the moss goes through before it can be bagged and shipped. Not only that, there was an excellent dock at Nikiski. The more I studied the opportunity and discussed it with possible investors the more feasible it appeared to be.

Next I requested a rate from the barge company that supplied most of the merchandise coming into the Kenai Peninsula and Anchorage. Their barges were fully loaded coming north, but went back to Seattle virtually empty. This looked like an excellent back haul for them. They should be able to give me a rate that would make our product competitive in the stateside market.

The shipping rate to Alaska has always been very high. Their response was that the rate was the same north or south. No, they would not negotiate. Bitter lesson number 13. The die was cast. I was out $5000 of my dwindling capital. We would return to civilization full time.

While I was involved in the pursuit of riches from a moss operation time ran out on the lease of our house. We could now re-occupy it and live a normal life. Problem was I had no job, we had not been in residence on the homestead for the required 14 months. That would not come until September 4th.

We remembered the plight of the Gilberts so it was a necessity for Bobbie to hold down the homestead until our time had expired. The children had to be in Anchorage to start school.

One day our old friend Bob Green landed on the lake. He was piloting Dean Springer around in Springer's new plane. They stayed for lunch then Springer offered me a job as Sales Manager for a Kitchen and Appliance Distributorship he was starting up.

As it worked out the children and I moved back to town, and Bobbie stayed on the homestead. A good friend and neighbor, whose children played with ours, was kind enough to move in with Bobbie for the duration of the required time. Now we applied for the patent on the land. A few months later we received it.

Ravens

Ravens were plentiful in the winter, both in town and on the homestead. We had watched the ravens tease our dog Pluto in town. He would go out on the Park Strip in front of our house and chase them. They played him for the fool by waiting for him to run close, then hop up and fly a short distance, land and wait. They would repeat this until ol' Pluto would get exhausted and give up. They are a very smart bird. My brother Dean fed the ravens in the winter. They would gather in his Balm of Gilead trees and squawk and chatter until he would scatter the stale bread that he got from the bakery. Dean told of watching one raven in the fall monitor a hornet's nest in one of the trees. The time came when the hornets, because of the cold became less and less active. When the cold finally stopped their activity altogether and they were in a stupor in the nest, the raven snipped the nest from the branch, followed it to the ground and calmly feasted on the dormant hornets. Here the ravens were a noisy nuisance and possibly an omen of darkness and despair.

"Quote the raven nevermore!" Edgar Allen Poe.

Sadly, that "nevermore" applies to our homestead. With the extension of the Hollywood Road, which was on our north section line we began the frustrating encounter with vandals. Up to that time, in the many years since we had obtained our patent on the land, we could leave the cabin unlocked and a fire set for anyone who happened by and needed shelter for a night of so. Bobbie had a month's supply of dried food stored in metal garbage cans for use in any disaster such as an earthquake or volcanic eruption. We had experienced both so she was prepared for emergency conditions. She had it so organized that all we needed to take for the weekend was fresh vegetables and meat.

The vandals stole or destroyed the food, stole the refrigerator, table, chairs, bedding, propane tanks, gas cook stove, and other goods that we had accumulated over the years. It got so that every time we went there for the weekend we had to spend all our time cleaning or repairing the place. Incredible cruelty on their part was the discovery of three mummified dogs that had been locked in the cabin to starve. Then, one winter they burnt the cabin down. Everything was lost.

Disheartened we tried to sell off some of the property, but had limited success. Finally, in 1997 the "Miller's Reach Fire," set by arsonists in a high wind, destroyed hundreds of acres. The spruce beetle had killed thousands of trees so the fire had unlimited dry fuel for it voracious appetite. It left blackened poles, standing at crazy angles where our forest had been. Our homestead was in the most devastated area.

My Gal

Would I do it all over again? Ask Bobbie to marry me? You bet your life I would! Many friends have told me that it was the smartest thing I ever did. Now who would know that better than I?

We met on a boat, going to Alaska, in 1940. We were on the boat for four days and in that time probably spent, at the least, eight or ten hours together. It was enough to shape our lives. We got together a few months later, courted for six months and then got married, 59 years ago.

Bobbie has been wife, lover, mother, partner and a great and cheerful companion. I appreciate all this more than I can ever express. From Trinidad to Nome we have been through blizzards, earthquakes, hurricanes, volcanic eruptions, tornadoes, fires, homesteading, wars, and more.

She presented me with four wonderful children who have given me the treasure of five lovely granddaughters, and a great grandson.

Bobbie was a loyal and faithful wife during the four and a half years I spent in the service. She was a loving, full-time parent to our children, and the effort she put into raising them is evident in the fine men and woman they turned out to be. I am very grateful to her for that effort.

A kind, gentle, lady with no pretensions, she is an easy companion in the calm periods, but a strong, steady supporter in times of stress. We've had our share of each. I have taken her on a roller coaster ride of at least 25 different jobs, positions, endeavors, pipe dreams and some real successes. We have had no money and plenty of money. We have taken cruises, gone to conventions, had jeeps, boats, airplanes, RVs, country cabins, and had a helluva lot of fun with them all with our children, grand-children, and now our great grandson. I am truly thankful!

I'm not sayin' she's a saint. Sometimes, well, sometimes she talks back!

The Jensen Story
September 20, 1957

When Tom shot the moose it was still on the beach but moving toward the water. The bullet entered the moose's head as he entered the lake, his charge carrying him over 100 feet before he died.

Tom and the three boys; Tommy 14, Timmy 9, and Freddie 5 had gone up to Healy Lake, off the Tanana River to a friend's cabin to hunt moose. Now they had a moose down, but a big problem. How to get the moose ashore so it could be dressed, quartered and hung.

The two Toms waded out and manhandled the moose toward shore. They were successful while the carcass would still float. When the antlers grabbed bottom it was stuck. They gave up. Going ashore they stretched out on the grass. "Damn, what now?"

"Tommy, take the boat and go back to the car. There is a Come-a-long in the trunk."

"Okay, dad."

"There is plenty of gas, you should make it in 3-3 1/2 hours."

Tommy jumped in the boat, was pushed off by Tom and the boys, cranked the motor and took off down the lake. Tom almost waved him back, but with luck everything would be all right. "I hope so, damn! I sure do hope so," he mumbled.

The car was twenty-five miles away. When Tommy was within nine or ten miles of it he cut around a bend, nearly striking a moose calf. Tommy idled the motor down and was enjoying the close contact with the calf, when he heard a splash. Coming from the right was mama moose. Tommy and the boat were between mother and calf, so he twisted the throttle; the bow raised then slammed down. A snag holed the bottom. As the water rushed in, Tommy cut for the bank and rammed the bow up on a gravel bar.

Stunned by what had happened, Tommy turned for help. There was none. "What do I do now? That damn hole is as big as a softball. It's high and dry, and there's nothing to patch it with." Picking up the bail can he started on the water. The dilemma diminished with each dip and splash. "Must be over half way to the car. Dip. Splash. We gotta have a boat. Dip. Splash. Better go to the car. Dip. Splash."

When the bottom was dry, he tilted the motor, jumped out of the boat, tied the bowline to a log and headed out. Beating his way through brush, slogging through swamps, crossing countless creeks, struggling over streams, rising over ridges, Tommy finally staggered up to the car. No license, but he could drive. He had a plan.

The trip to Delta Junction was forty miles. The people at the service station treated him to a nice dinner and gave him some fiberglass patch material for the boat. Next Tommy called Tundra Topics, a message program aired by a Fairbanks radio station. Every night at 9 PM they would broadcast messages to the people in the Bush Country from friends and relatives, a vital service to Alaskans living in isolation.

"To Tom Jensen at Healy Lake. Tommy had boat trouble, but will be back tomorrow."

The people at the service station put Tommy up for the night. He hit the kip early. Back at the lake the hours dragged by. Time for his return came, but no Tommy. Tom worried as more hours slipped past. He had to do something.

"Boys! (To Tim and Freddie) I'm going to take this canoe, go across to Krickstaders, and ask him to take his boat and help us find Tommy. You kids stay right here at the cabin. I will be back as soon as I can." The Krickstaders were homesteaders. They were the only other people on the lake.

Tom took his rifle, launched the derelict canoe he had found on the bank, and headed across the lake. By this time it was nearly six o'clock, almost dusk. Tom was three quarters of the way across the lake when he decided to sit rather than kneel. In making the shift he lost his balance, the canoe overturned.

Though he was warmly dressed in woolen long underwear, pants, shirt, jacket, and burdened with rubber hip boots, he was able to surface and grab the canoe. With much effort he was able to turn the canoe right side up. After several futile attempts to get back inside, he abandoned that idea. Guiding the canoe and kicking, near complete exhaustion, he was approaching shore. Suddenly the canoe caught the current from an incoming stream. He and the canoe were pushed back out into the main body of the lake. Bitterly cold from the 40-degree water, hands numb from clutching the canoe, Tom continued to fight the current, trying to get ashore.

Nine o'clock came and Tundra Topics aired the first message from Tommy to Tom. Tim and Freddie were worried, frightened and terribly alone. Tom was struggling for his life in the lake and wondering, "Where's my son?"

Mrs. Krickstader, listening to Tundra Topics, wondered if she shouldn't tell Paul about the message to Healy Lake. The announcer came on again. "I normally do not do this, but I will repeat the message to Tom Jensen at Healy Lake. Tommy had boat trouble and will be back tomorrow."

Mrs. Krickstader thought, "I'd better tell Paul."

Finding Paul in the woodshed she gave him the message.

"I had better run over there and see if they heard it."

Tim and Freddie rushed down to the beach as Paul landed.

"Where's your Dad?"

"We don't know, he got in the canoe to come see you."

"How long ago?"

"Long, long time ago."

"You kids hop in the boat." They did and Paul started back across the lake.

By this time darkness had fallen. Paul could see nothing but indistinct shapes on an obscure shoreline. Halfway across he stopped the engine to listen.

Tom, paralyzed with cold and exhaustion, could not push anymore. All he was capable of was to hang onto the canoe.

When Paul had first started his motor to go to the Jensen cabin, Tom got a lift of spirit. He yelled to Paul as he passed by, but of course, Paul couldn't hear him. Now Tom had nothing left. All he could think of was his boys. He had called again when the motor stopped at the cabin, but there was no power in his voice and they didn't hear him.

When the motor stopped, this time, the incredible stillness of the wild country settled over the lake. Tom tried again. "Help! Help!" Though his voice was weak, sound carries well over water and he was heard.

Paul cranked up the motor, they found Tom, and pulled him into the boat. He had been in the frigid water for 3 1/2 hours.

"Tommy had boat trouble. Sent a Tundra Topics message that he would be back tomorrow."

"Thank God he's alright."

Tom was shivering uncontrollably so Paul raced the boat to Jensen's cabin. Tom was stripped down, dried off, then wrapped in blankets and sleeping bags but he could not stop shivering. Tom drank over a quart of Seagram's whiskey and eventually went to sleep.

The morning of the twenty-first Tommy drove back to the river, took the Come-a-long and the fiberglass patching material and headed for the boat. The same creeks and swamps had to be overcome, but now he was an experienced woodsman. Arriving back at the boat he hitched the Come-a-long to the bow ring, the other end to a snag and winched the boat onto a log, where he could work on the bottom. Using the fiberglass cloth, Epoxy and some birch bark, he contrived a makeshift repair.

After the quick drying Epoxy had set, Tommy launched the boat, checked for leaks, and hoping for the best headed up river to the camp. Opening the army musette bag the service station lady had given him to carry the patching materials, he removed sandwiches, an apple and some carrots she had packed for him. Though the trip was boring he munched away the miles back to the camp.

Back at the cabin, Paul was checking on Tom, who was still exhausted, had a tremendous hangover, but seemed to be recovering.

At three PM Tommy arrived. The two Toms were reserved as Tommy beached the boat, each struggling with guilt. Tommy for punching a hole in the bottom of his Dad's boat. Tom for sending his boy on a man-sized mission.

"Hi Dad!"

"What happened?"

"I put a hole in the boat. Had to get some patching."

"Well, you had better get some food, then we'll get to work.

"I had...O.K. Dad."

Tommy left for the cabin just as Paul arrived.

"I see the boy got back. What happened?"

"Knocked a hole in the bottom! Kids!"

"Well Tom, we best get to work and take care of that meat."

With his help the work started. They attached the Come-a-long to the moose and a tree, and dragged the moose up on the beach. The two men and the boy, gutted, quartered, and hung it on the meat rack. Hard work, but a simple chore for experienced hands. MISSION ACCOMPLISHED!

Epilogue

Health scientists now know that alcohol is not a proper treatment for hypothermia. In fact they can quote many cases where it was fatal when used. Tom certainly had hypothermia, although this incident occurred long before that term was in common usage. Tom believed that it was the heavy woolen clothing that kept him warm enough to survive.

"Why didn't Tom die from the heavy dose of alcohol?" While you're pondering that, ask this. "Why didn't Tom drown?"

Peyton

Peyton was standing in the door of his cabin when the helicopter landed. Three guys descended but the pilot remained aboard. Of the six cabins on the mouth of the river, no one else paid any attention to the intrusion. The fishing season was over and all the fishermen were putting the set-net sites in order for the winter.

Peyton strolled over. "Hi Guys! What's up?"

"We're with Saturn Geophysical and are going to be checking this area for possible oil deposits. We need a base so are looking around for a site. We thought this might be suitable. Is this area available?"

"Could be, I've got five acres here. We could possibly make a deal. Come over to the cabin and we'll talk."

The three trudged over to the cabin. Peyton offered them a beer, pop or coffee. When they were all settled the leader said. "I am George Hampton. This is Harry and Dave. We are Petroleum Engineers assigned to sound this area for oil deposits. We need a site on the water where we can fly in temporary housing, a freezer and cook tent. We will have five people. We will drill a well for fresh water and figure on staying for up to six months.

Peyton could see a shower of hundred dollar bills descending, so offered his site and services. A deal was quickly struck with Peyton getting $150.00 a day for the site. He would acquire the fifty cubic foot freezer and, of course, the well they would drill. In addition they chartered Peyton's 27 foot dory with him as skipper for an additional $350.00 per day.

Within ten days the camp was set up, the well drilled (turned out to be artesian) and they were fully operational.

Peyton, or his buddy Chris, piloted the engineers around Cook Inlet while they set off their explosive charges, and recorded the data. With the weather getting steadily worse, George began to complain about the dory. He felt it was inadequate for the work they were doing. "We need something larger, more stable, with some shelter on it," he said.

Peyton took some time off, leaving Chris to squire the crew around. He went into Anchorage, got on the phone and finally found a 73 foot LCM, (War Surplus Power Barge) for sale in Homer. Peyton flew down, found the barge, named Dora, and the owner, Hap Oliver. He inspected it and was pleased that it was a sound vessel with good engines. It looked really shipshape.

"The ad said you wanted $19,000.00 for it. That right?"

"For cash I'll come down to seventeen-five, but it has to be soon!"

"I'll see what I can do." They shook hands and parted. Peyton flew back to camp.

The next time Hampton bitched about the dory and longed for a bigger craft, Peyton said, "Well I've got an LCM, but it's tied up for a while, that's why I didn't mention it. Be free in three or four weeks, if you want something that big?"

"How big is it?"

"Seventy feet or so."

"Could we see it?"

"Sure, how about day after tomorrow?"

"I can make that."

Peyton takes Chris aside, "I want you to go down to Homer. Get acquainted with the caretaker on the Dora. When George and I come down to let him inspect it, I want that guy in town out of the way. Be able to buy him a beer or a broad, whatever it takes to clear the deck. OK?" Peyton gives Chris three one hundred-dollar bills.

The day for the inspection arrived. Peyton and George flew

down to Homer. They leisurely inspected the ship. Chris had done his job. George was satisfied. There was a crude pilothouse, a propane burner, small gas refrigerator, small sink, emergency gear, head, etc.

"Looks good to me. How much a day do you want?"

"How about six hundred a day, that includes me or Chris?"

"Yeah, that's all right. I'll have the papers drawn up."

They went to get something to eat. By incredible coincidence Chris was there. They joined him at his table.

After they had eaten, Peyton asked Chris, "Would you mind going back to camp with George? I have to try to collect some money a guy owes me for over two years now. I'll be back tomorrow."

George and Chris leave. Peyton chases down Hap Oliver and gives him a check for twenty-five hundred dollars, as earnest money. This done he goes to the bank with the papers and asks to be financed for the purchase of the boat.

"Sure, no problem. Just bring in the contract."

"Thank you very, very much SIR!" Peyton goes back to camp.

Work goes on. After a week, George says, "Peyton, the contract is drawn up at the office in Anchorage, ready for you to sign."

Big sigh. "Great, I'll go in tomorrow and do that."

Peyton goes to Anchorage, signs the contract to provide a ship that he does not own, by October first. His month has slipped away. He has just six days to wrap it all up. He takes his copy, and flies down to Homer.

The caretaker of the Dora tells him, "Oh! Hap flew to Hawaii. Got hold of some money, somehow, just took off, like that!" He snaps his fingers.

"When will he be back?"

"Didn't say."

"Where can I reach him?"

"Don't know."

"Who would know?"

"Don't know. Maybe Gladys!"

"Gladys who?"

"Don't know."

"Where can I find her?"

"White house, Third and Taylor."

"I'll give you twenty dollars to take me there."

"OK." They get in an old pickup. No one is home at Third and Taylor.

Peyton goes next door. He knocks, the door opens a bit and a ladies face appeared.

"Can you tell me where Gladys is?"

"She went to Hawaii."

"Know where she'll be staying?"

"Nope."

Peyton gives his guide a twenty, and they go back to town. Crushed, Peyton leans against a building. "What in hell am I going to do now?" Some people walk by, chattering. They turn into the building. Peyton sees it is a bar.

"Maybe a drink will clear my head! Gotta think, Damn!"

Three days later, Chris tells George.

"I need to go to town. Can't figure where Peyton is!"

"That's OK, Chris. We have a lot of paper work to catch up on. Go ahead."

Chris finds Peyton in their favorite bar in Homer, in no condition to discuss anything. He gets a motel room and puts Peyton to bed.

"What the hell do I do now? Can't stay here, got to get back to drive George and the boys around. Can't leave this jerk here. Cripes! The dumb ass. Why did he do this?"

Chris leaves a sign on the dresser. "CALL ME BEFORE YOU DO ANYTHING! Chris."

Peyton emerges from his stupor. He showers, gets dressed then goes to a cafe. After five cups of coffee, potatoes and eggs he flies back to camp. He has decided to make a clean breast of it all to Hampton.

"George, I have a confession to make. I cannot deliver the LCM as we agreed on. It's a long story. I don't really own the ship. I was going to buy it if I got a contract with you. Now I can't deliver. The owner has disappeared. There is no way I can complete the deal."

George looked at Peyton. The longer he remained silent, the more Peyton squirmed. When his head was almost to his knees, George said.

"I knew you didn't own it!"

"You knew it?"

"Watched the whole scam. You are one lousy con man. Claimed the ship was under contract. Hell, it hadn't been used in weeks. Now you've found a conscience." He paused then continued. "Don't worry about it, it's OK."

In the quiet, after this exchange, the radio became audible.

"There was an accident near Soldotna that injured three people. Hap Oliver and Gladys Knight were injured when their Plymouth Caravan was struck by a teenage driver in a Ford pickup. They were taken to the Valley Hospital but then released. The teenager is being held, pending further investigation.

"That's him! THAT'S HIM! Peyton jumped from his chair. "Gawd! If I had only kept my mouth SHUT! Damn!"

"Relax! Relax!" George was smiling. "Go get him, we still have a deal. It's only money."

Lane

The telephone rings. "Don! It's Lane!"

God! Now what? "Hi Lane."

"Don. You know I've really screwed up. I need to talk to you. I'm going to kill myself!"

Kill? Kill—the word burgeoned into a steel claw, clutching my heart. I felt like a stone statue. I could barely breath, let alone respond.

Time ticked on-- then

"Christ, Lane! You can't do that. Think about it!"

"I have Don. That's all I think about. Jane's going to divorce me. She won't even talk to me. I'll lose my kids. God, I miss them. I feel like I'm in a hole with no bottom, hanging on but not for long. I need you to come over. Now!"

The dilemma was a leaden shroud that descended and enveloped me, no opening for insight or solution to enter.

Jane and Lane had been our neighbors. It had developed into a friendship. We had picnicked, partied, and had a lot of fun together. Lane was good looking, good natured, good company. He and I were veterans, hunters, and building our houses with no money. We had four kids. They also had four with another on the way. Jane had taken the kids to her folks in Sacramento and then filed for divorce.

The trouble had started when Lane quit his very good job as a telephone lineman, bought a truck and started a hauling business. He had made this change because his brother-in-law had started one and was phenomenally successful. Lane failed and couldn't handle the failure. He started drinking more and, I suspected, was using drugs.

After Jane left, some of Lane's new friends conned him into letting them run a poker game at his house. He bragged to me about getting a percentage. Later, a hooker moved in with him. Helped him down the tube.

"Don! You can talk to Jane. You and Bobbie can help me get her back!"

"We've tried, Lane! You know that!"

Jane had come back to finalize the divorce and stayed with us. She wouldn't talk to Lane, or to us, about him. Lane would call, pleading with us to help him. The calls continued. We would repeat our advice as to how he should win Jane back, then this bitch he was shacking up with would come on another line, cuss us out, calling us all kinds of filthy names and tell us to mind our own goddam business.

"You've got to throw that bitch, and all the rest of them out!"

"I've already done that. I need you to come over and talk to me. Now!"

"Okay! I'll come."

Lane's house was a daylight basement of concrete blocks with a temporary tarpaper roof on what would be the first floor. No moon, stars or snow to lend light, it loomed in the night projecting only fear and foreboding. Crossing the yard, I opened the door and stepped into the dark utility room. The door to the living quarters, ajar, allowed faint light to enter my space. I walked over to the door, pushed it open and stopped. Lane, in silhouette, the picture window behind him, sat facing me. On his knees his 30-06 moose rifle.

"Hi! Thanks for coming over."

"Hi! Let's have some light?"

"No!"

"Lane, you can't do this. My God, you just can't. What you have to do is get your life back together. I'm glad you got rid of those bastards you had in here. That's a good start. Here, let me take the gun!"

"Don't! Don, how did all this happen? How could I screw everything up, like this? I can't believe it. She won't even talk to me. I call her folks but she won't come to the phone. When she was at your place she wouldn't see me. I've really lost it!"

"We've tried. We couldn't get her to talk to you, or even to us about you."

While Jane was with us, Lane sneaked into our house. He hid under the steps in our laundry room. Jane was living in our basement apartment. Bobbie had heard a sound and went down into the utility room to check it out. As she approached the laundry trays she could see, out of the corner of her eye, Lane crouched in the dark under the stairs. He had a pistol in his hand. Bobbie deliberately turned away, did some busy work in the room, then, though terrified, went back up stairs.

When I investigated I found Lane, with a pistol, crouching in the dark. The adrenaline shock finally subsided enough for me to speak. "Come on out Lane! I have to know what you are doing here." He was drunk. I never challenged him about the gun. He did put it behind his belt, in front.

"I have to see Jane!"

"She isn't staying here any more." (She was over visiting her sister.) He was actually ashamed. I could tell. I was finally able to get him to leave.

We sat for a while. By that time I could see his features fairly well. His face was a mask of misery.

"Remember when we helped that joker carry out his moose? Must have been two miles. First load we walked for forty-five minutes then Dean called out. "Hey guys, there's a moose kill over there." We went over and it was our kill. We had walked in a big circle. Ha! Ha!"

Lane didn't respond.

"Then there was the time you wanted us to homestead the intersection at Glenallen. We would have had all three corners.

Nothing has happened there. We would have starved. Would have been a real screwup."

"Not as big as this one!"

"Then there was that fight at the Silver Dollar ba..."

"Knock it off! Don, what am I going to do?"

"Lane, I only know you have to start over. Get back on your feet, off the booze. Be like you were before. Once you get going again, get your old job back, go out and see Jane. She'll be there! You're going to have to court her like you did when you first met. Win her back! To me, that seems the only way. You've already made a start!"

Silence again. I sat there in the dark, in a stupor of despair and dubiety. No use going for the gun. He was as strong as I was, and desperate. Death was on his mind. Mine too. Talk him out of it? Maybe. He was agreeing with me some, but his emotions were controlling, not his reason. I felt overwhelmed with futility.

"You say you want your family back. What are you willing to give up to get them?"

"Everything! Dammit, everything! Nothing else is important to me!"

"Can you really do that?"

"I can! I have to get them back. Without them, there is nothing. Now, I know that!'"

"Okay, we can tell her. It may be a while before she will listen, but I'm sure she is praying for the old Lane to return. We'll help all we can, once we see a change. Something to report to her."

That somber silence returned. He sat, immobile, for several minutes then he said. "Okay! That's what I'll do. God, I'd give anything to get back to the way it was. You and Bobbie, Dean and Betty, Dan and Millie, Jane and I."

"You can do it! If you go straight, she will know about it. We'll help!"

No response. I broke the stygian stillness with, "Well I have to be going. Work tomorrow. Want the light on?'

"Naw, just leave it off. Thanks for coming."

"You okay?"

"Yeah, I'm all right." No handshake offered.

I headed for the utility room. My back wanted to beat me out the door. That damn rifle was still on his knees.

On the ride home I could breathe again. I felt the leaden shroud begin to shrivel. He had accepted my plan. It made sense. He could make it happen. Another problem solved.

Jane stayed with us, for the funeral.

Terror

I know about terror, hopeless terror, and will-paralyzing terror. It knifed into my being when I was 14 years old.

I was the youngest of 5 children, four boys and a girl. We were raised in a mining town in Utah. When the '29 stock market crash came, Dad lost his garage business. Wiped out. Being an ex-miner, before his business life, he knew the short life span of the young men who worked in the mines.

"Not for my boys!" Dad decided. We moved to Salt Lake City as strangers with no connections to help us fit into a new way of life. We struggled for an existence. I went through junior high. My sister and I worked in a dance hall 'til two thirty, three nights a week. Then we six moved to San Francisco where my oldest brother, Lisle, was an accountant for General Motors. He had told Mom and Dad, in letters, that he was working, very hard at night, on a new system of accounting for the dealer branches and felt that he was nearing completion of the task. It would be very important to his career.

This move was a disaster. Whether or not it was the cause of Lisle's breakdown, it certainly contributed to his problem. It was my initiation into gut wrenching fear.

Lisle was the crown prince of our family, a college graduate, smart, handsome, great physique, imperious. He was the oldest. Mom and Dad beamed with pride when telling of his accomplishments, which were many. Officer in the Military Reserve, musician, great athlete, sharp accountant among them. He was ten years older than I was, so our relationship was casual, unemotional. He was an example I was expected to imitate. The only time that I remember him paying attention to me was when I was five and he taught me to sing my first song. "Doodle-dee-doo."

The picture I have in my mind of our arrival in San Francisco is a dark fear driven spectacle of Dad and Mom and the rest of us trying to cope with a situation we could not begin to understand and accept. Our flat was, dimly lighted, strange, depressing and cold, with no family warmth or feeling. The constant fog seemed to penetrate the walls to add dismal dampness to our confusion. We milled around, each in our own orbit of despair.

Lisle had a "nervous breakdown" as it was then called. I knew only that Dad was crushed. He was floundering, desperately trying to put our shattered world back to some semblance of emotional stability. Lisle was a stricken, confused, coldly obstinate man. He refused all attempts, by my Mother and Dad, to get help for him.

Lisle disappeared from our flat. Now the tension and frantic efforts to "do something" filled the rooms with doom and hopeless foreboding. After an agonizing week of worry, the police picked Lisle up, wandering down the railroad tracks in San Jose. He was confused, disoriented, and irrational, and was being held in jail there.

I was not part of any of the interplay that took place. I was lost in wonder at what had happened to our idol and why this situation had descended on our family. Later I learned that Lisle had been placed in an institution. "Dementia Praecox Paranoia" was the diagnosis of his condition. That, strangely chilling, unknown description of his problem increased my bewilderment. No one counseled me on what had happened, what was being done. I was buffeted by the reactions of my parents and older brothers. My sister, two years older than I, knew as little as I did. I became more and more confused and lost. For me, a soul searing experience.

Our life settled into a more reasonable routine. Now Mom, Dad and my older brothers had to plan what to do. Lisle's job had vanished so we had no income. In the midst of the great depression this was a disaster. The decision was made to move to Berkeley. There we managed to survive and later made our move to Alaska.

Just before leaving for Alaska my boxing coach's wife offered to tell me my fortune. I relcuntly let her do so. She ruptured my resolve with a devastating declaration. "You will, at the age of fifty five, enter an institution for the remainder of your life." Although I didn't believe in fortune tellers that little nugget of negativity was always in the back of my mind for the next thirty seven years.

My emotional burden eased, but the terrible, numbing fear I carried submerged, would surface with a paralyzing grip on my vitals. Would I, too, suffer the ordeal of my brother? Why had it happened, what was the cause, when would it hit me. It wasn't fair. There was no answer. The question "What about me—my future?" The dreaded hand of the unknown would clutch my heart and leave me gasping.

For six years the black shroud of hopelessness would descend and engulf my soul. Terrified inside, I had to show a calm I did not feel, strength I did not have and attitude that was only on the surface. Work, duty and companionship would gradually bring me to a brooding, near normality. I talked to no one about the problem.

Lisle was put through treatments. Electric shock, pills, sedatives, threatened lobotomy, (Christ, they were going to remove one lobe of his brain. They figured that this would help him?) And God knows what else without Lisle ever voicing any comment on his experience. He communicated not at all, mostly showing a cold reserve to all of us. He did improve. After a while he was able to work for several years as a chainman for a surveyor. He helped survey the boundaries for Mt. McKinley National Park. His boss and mentor, a wonderful man, was working with Lisle, encouraging, counseling and apparently caring. We could see improvement when Lisle returned at the end of the season. Unfortunately, the man committed suicide during the winter so Lisle lost again, both his job and his friend.

I witnessed his partial return to a normal life. All this did little to resolve my dilemma. My salvation came when, in the throes of a great, deep well of depression I was suddenly impaled by a shaft of fear, pinned, struggling, to a wall of doubt. Desperate, I said "God, I can run no more! I cannot solve this. I am, now, placing it all in your hands!"

I immediately felt a comforting mantel of peace descending, enveloping my whole being. I now understand the meaning of a blessing. Since that moment I have no doubt whatever about the existence of a Supreme Being.

Psychiatrists may try to explain this away in their fashion. Means nothing to me. I was there. It happened. I was blessed and at 81 am still living the wonderment of a healthy, happy existence.

Earline's World

April 5, 1895 George and Genevieve Campbell had just become parents of Earline Genevieve Campbell. As Genevieve (Jenny) held the newborn infant, she wondered, would Earline, in her life, experience an event equal to the funeral of Abraham Lincoln, which Jenny had attended, as a child.

The world was being changed by events that same year. The first pneumatic tires were used on vehicles. X-rays were utilized in medicine, and the first motorist fatality occurred. An electric starter for engines was invented and steel frame buildings were introduced.

1897 Earline was two and busy exploring her world. Elsewhere, the first commercial radio station appeared, the baby incubator, radio distress signal, woman car driver and news film followed.

1901 "REMEMBER THE MAINE," The Spanish American War, Teddy Roosevelt and the Rough Riders. Earline, six years old, had just arrived in Port Angeles, Washington with her Mother, her sister Emily 7, brothers Francis 12 and Alfred 14. They had preceded their father who had stayed in Harvey Illinois to sell the home and possessions. The family's aim was to homestead.

1906 The horseless carriage would change her life, but right away, powered flight, a stunt that would later explode into an industry was sharing growing pains with Earline. The Panama Canal was completed.

The Campbell homestead chores and going to school kept the girls busy, dawn to dark. The large living room with its tongue and groove floor made it the neighborhood-gathering place for parties and dances. They still had time to climb to the top of Blue Mountain to camp out.

The Ottoman Empire crumbled in Europe. Earline quit school after grade eight.

1910 Alfred and Francis bought a sawmill on the Elwa River. Earline and Emily cooked, baked bread, cut wood, and carried water through bear territory for the brothers and crew.

1914 Earline meet handsome Jim Jacobs, a forest Ranger and they eloped to Seattle and were married.

Archduke Ferdinand was assassinated and World War I erupted.

Earline's first-born Dalmain entered the world. Francis transformed from logger to ambulance driver in far off France.

1916 Daughter Alice was born to the Jacobs. Earline became a Charter Member of the Fairview Grange.

1918 The Allies won the war. A gal chopped up some saloons with her little hatchet and Congress declared Prohibition.

Enter the wild, exciting twenties. Caruso was the world's greatest Tenor. America allowed women to vote and son Robert arrived to join the Jacobs youngsters. Jim was still a Ranger and they were living on the old Jacobs homestead.

The model T Ford was the most popular car in the country. Grandpa Hile Jacobs couldn't handle one. It wouldn't 'gee;' it wouldn't 'haw;' and it wouldn't 'whoa.' He wound up stump stopped. Gangster wars, Broadway shows, Hollywood movies occupied the attention of many, but the Jacobs family mourned the loss of newborn, Bernice in 1926.

Prohibition wasn't working. Bootlegging was rampant and people were getting rich trading on the stock market until...

1929 They called it the "THE CRASH." Speculators were jumping from skyscrapers to their deaths. Corporations failed and the unemployed were in the breadlines. The great "Depression" had started. Hoover was helpless. Jim was longshoring and Earline was doing housework.

Franklin Roosevelt, the sire of Mammoth Government started transferring American Taxpayers money to anyone and everyone, everywhere. The Jacobs family, with everyone else, struggled to eat and live.

1934 Earline had her first baby to be born in a hospital, his name is Donald. Jim was working on building highway 101 for 50 cents a day.

In Germany, Hitler was expanding his power, and took the Rhineland. Russia and Germany signed a Pact, Japan invaded China, Germany wins the Balkans and Italy seized Ethiopia.

Earline's concern is not world problems, but the nurturing and providing for her family. It was never easy, but she could and did do it. No quit in this gal. Son Dalmain marries Leila. Bob goes into the Navy.

December 7, 1941 "PEARL HARBOR." America enters wars in Europe and Asia. Battle after battle—Midway, Iwo Jima, Normandy, Battle of the Bulge, Tobruk, El Alemein, North Africa. Who can remember the order? Daughter Alice married John and has children. Earline works in shipyard building barges.

1943 Earline buys house on Peabody Street in Port Angeles.

1945 Germany surrenders. Truman drops the A-bomb. Japan quits. Earline is working in Angeles Creamery.

1951 America suffers Korean War.

1955 Earline takes her first plane ride and is thrilled by the flight to Anchorage and back. She could not be talked into becoming an Alaskan.

Don completed his two years in the Navy.

Ghandi is killed. The H-bomb is exploded. Stalin dies. Sputnik, product of German Rocket Scientists, working for Russia, launches Space Age. Jenny Campbell dies at age 103.

Vietnam, a terrible war sacrificed thousand of American youth for no good reason.

Earline is retired, and has time to visit family and friends.

Nixon resigns. There is a worldwide recession. Russia invades Afghanistan. Iran and Iraq fight several years to no decision.

Reagan makes a believer out of Russia. They crumble, and the Berlin wall comes down.

Earline is giver a plaque for quilting 2000 lap robes for the "KIDS" in the Nursing Homes. Earline is 95.

Now 100 years old Earline has seen transportation progress from the horse and wagon to supersonic jets and rockets to the moon and beyond. Medicine is capable of heart and lung transplants, brain surgery and other miracles. Communication has gone from telegraph, the hand cranked telephone to instant electronic, worldwide, contact.

The thing that hasn't changed is human nature. Some people are very bad; most are good. Earline is one of the best. Amidst all the greed, violence and frailties of the world leaders and people, Earline is steadfast, honest, capable and self-sufficient. Hers is a life of discipline, self-reliance and love for family and friends. Earline's creed is "Don't do anything you wouldn't do if you were in Heaven. That's the way I see it. It works for me."

Lifetide

I saw him slip. He was sliding back down the side of the fairly steep, little gully when he fell forward. His shotgun, lying flat, kept his right arm from going into the mud, but his left hand went in beyond his wrist. Sliding, on his knees, his feet soon hit the small stream. Both hands on the gun he pushed, buried it, but struggled erect. Now his feet started to sink into the slick, gray goo the mud had become. His weight and the silent struggle to free his feet caused him to sink deeper, one foot at a time, into the clutching gray mass.

Alaska's Cook Inlet clay, a gray glacial silt that forms so much of the Cook Inlet basin, has captured and drowned, many a duck hunter, fisherman, four wheeler, or other pilgrim, over the years. The silt is so fine that a glass of water from the Matanuska River will not settle all the fines, sometimes for several days. The thing that makes it so very treacherous is the fact that the tides, up to forty feet at times, can rise and drown the hapless, trapped one, before a rescue can be effected.

It is impossible to pull a person out of the mud if their legs are in very deep. The suction is so strong that the body would be pulled apart. The only way to break this suction is by forcing air down around the limbs. There is no practical way to do this without the special equipment available only from the Anchorage Fire Department, or the Paramedics stationed at Girdwood, on the Turnagain Arm.

The physical properties of the clay are extraordinary. You can grab a lump, which appears reasonably solid, squash it several times in your hands and it will liquefy to the point where it will run out between your fingers. This characteristic caused the tremendous loss of houses and lives during the 1964 Earthquake in Anchorage, Alaska. Many homes were built on land that had a layer of this clay forty or fifty feet below the surface. When the earth continued to shake for several minutes, the layer of gravel, above this liquefied clay, was forced by the wave action of the earthquake, to slide to the north as far as a quarter of a mile, to the bluff overlooking Cook Inlet. Many houses and people took this terrible ride and toppled into the water.

I watched, helpless to help, as he continued to struggle. I started toward him but he shouted, "No! STAY BACK! ONE IS ENOUGH! YOU CAN'T DO ANY GOOD!" He was right, the steep sides of the gully allowed no footing. He had proven that. He was sinking slowly while the tide was bringing the water, inexorably, nearer.

Near complete exhaustion, he quit the struggle. He bowed his head. I closed my tear filled, eyes and whispered, "Our Father which art..." When I finished and looked up he was watching me. "You'd better get around that gut before the water gets any higher. At least someone will know what's happened."

"I CAN'T LEAVE YOU!"

"You wanna die? YOU WANNA DIE? I DON'T! DAMMIT! YOU DON'T HAVE TO! GET GOING!

He was right. He was always right. I started, then turned. He waved me on.

"Tell Mindy I love her!"

I trudged away, wearing the leaden cloak of futility, the mantle of misery, that had first enveloped me when I realized there was no help and no hope.

When I turned again he was watching the water.

Later, looking back, one last time, I could not see him.

My smothered soul, struggling for survival with each reluctant step, eventually, made it back around the gut to good going. It changed nothing. It was a suddenly obscene scene of miles of hard packed earth.